מסורה
ArtScroll Series®

Rabbi Nosson Scherman / Rabbi Meir Zlotowitz

General Editors

IN

*Small things you can do
to make you feel so much better*

Published by

Mesorah Publications, ltd

JOY

A little inner joy
goes a long way

Roiza D. Weinreich

FIRST EDITION
First Impression . . . December 1993

Published and Distributed by
MESORAH PUBLICATIONS, Ltd.
Brooklyn, New York 11232

Distributed in Israel by
MESORAH MAFITZIM / J. GROSSMAN
Rechov Harav Uziel 117
Jerusalem, Israel

Distributed in Australia & New Zealand by
GOLD'S BOOK & GIFT CO.
36 William Street
Balaclava 3183, Vic., Australia

Distributed in Europe by
J. LEHMANN HEBREW BOOKSELLERS
20 Cambridge Terrace
Gateshead, Tyne and Wear
England NE8 1RP

Distributed in South Africa by
KOLLEL BOOKSHOP
22 Muller Street
Yeoville 2198, Johannesburg
South Africa

Printed in the United States of America by Noble Book Press Corp.
Bound by Sefercraft Quality Bookbinders, Ltd., Brooklyn, N.Y.

Not so long ago there was a little town in Poland called Trovitz. My great uncle, Harav Mordechai Nota Ackerman, was the Rav there. With warmth, humility and fatherly love, he united the Jewish families with their Father above.

From neighboring towns people travelled to settle their business quarrels. He showed both parties, with gentle friendliness, through parables and Talmudic quotes, that the Torah way is best.

Each week he walked to the main street dressed in Shabbos clothes to remind storekeepers to close their stores before Shabbos. "Alter, Ephraim, Yaakov Yosef, enough," he would call. "You've worked enough. Now is the time to live! Shabbos!"

He learned Torah each morning and every afternoon. His door was always open. His velvet eyes looked right into your soul. He knew each person's heart and solved each person's problem with a pure, gentle smile on his lips.

What little town did your parents come from?

Who were your ancestors?

Your ancestors and mine.

They are not gone.

They live on — in our Shabbos
in our Torah
in our kind acts
and in our gentle smiles.

Acknowledgements

I'd like to thank the many people who provided ideas and support during the process of writing this book.

My sincere thanks to Rabbi Ezriel Tauber who carefully reviewed the manuscript and added immeasurably to it. My appreciation goes to Esther Strong, Surie Gottesman, Chaia Erblich, Esther Press, Miriam Kaufman, Georgie Klein, Yiska Gross, Goldie Miller, Basy Berg, and Rebbitzen Carlbach for contributing carefully thought-out ideas and suggestions. Thanks especially to all the family members who contributed, including Chaim Weinreich, Yossie and Fern Weinreich, Yitzchok and Malka Sara Weinreich, Naftali Perlman, Shloime Perlman, Michael and Barbara Kesler, Sheah and Chaya Suri Friedman, and Motel and Manya Fisher.

My students at the Tuesday Tehillim class and the subscribers to my newsletter contributed most of the examples in the book. Henya Novick read the first draft and gave valuable recommendations. Once again, Fayge Silverman was thorough yet gentle with editing. She was patient and persistent in fitting all the parts together and made important creative contributions. Our friendship has deepened during our work together.

Gratitude goes to Rabbis Meir Zlotowitz and Nosson Scherman for putting their faith in this project. My special thanks to Rabbi Sheah Brander, whose expert knowledge made the book complete. My sincere appreciation to Mrs. Judi Dick for her encouragement, as well as to Mrs. Faigie Weinbaum, Mrs. Ethel Gottlieb, Chava Shulman, Mrs. Bassie Gutman,

Yehuda Gordon, Nichie Fendrich, and Mrs. Mindy Breier of the ArtScroll staff. I consider it a privilege to participate in the ArtScroll Series.

The first one to read significant portions of the book was my husband, Faivel. Since then he has helped me decide many times what will work and what won't and has patiently encouraged me not to give up when I faced minor setbacks. My parents, Mr. and Mrs. Moshe Perlman, and my mother-in-law, Mrs. Pearl Weinreich, have encouraged and supported all my various undertakings. I hope they will always have *nachas* from all their children and grandchildren.

The inspiration for this book was the example of my great-uncle, Chaim ben Naftali Binyomin, *zichrono livracha*. He had many reasons to complain, yet his greatness was that he always smiled gently instead. He was truly interested in others and understood how to make them feel better. He was a master of the lost art of doing what you can with what you have at all times.

I thank Hashem again for the wide acceptance of my first book and for the *zechus* of reaching thousands of people around the world with Torah ideas that have hopefully helped them to become better Jews.

וִיהִי נֹעַם ה׳ אֱלֹקֵינוּ עָלֵינוּ

וּמַעֲשֵׂה יָדֵינוּ כּוֹנְנָה עָלֵינוּ וּמַעֲשֵׂה יָדֵינוּ כּוֹנְנֵהוּ

May Hashem's Presence and Satisfaction rest upon us. May Hashem complete our efforts and assure their success. May the work of our hands establish Hashem's Kingdom on earth. (Tehillim 90:17).

1270 48ᵗʰ STREET
BROOKLYN, N.Y. 11219

Foreword

by Rabbi Ezriel Tauber

I am extremely happy to see this second book by Mrs. Roiza Weinreich. It proves that when a person has the proper attitude and *hashkafa,* nothing stands in the way. For although she is a busy mother with small children, managing a large household, she still finds the time to write books — and not only to write books, but to lecture, and help others to deal and cope, in the most practical ways, with everyday life. An accomplishment like that is only possible if one has truly internalized the Torah *hashkafa* on life, and reading between the lines of this book one can plainly see that Mrs. Weinreich is not only teaching that *hashkafa,* but also living it. This book, therefore, stands as an example to everyone of how the Torah *hashkafa* — particularly of seeing meaningfulness in every event — not only helps in coping with life but produces an excitement toward living which is powerful enough to overcome any obstacle.

Therefore, may Hashem help the author to see much *nachas* from her works. And may she continue to be a shining example to others, showing that even a busy mother can still reach outside her home and affect many lives. I wish her the best.

Table of Contents

A Little Inner Joy Goes a Long Way

Torah is accompanied by a supernatural guarantee: We are assured that our every small effort is blessed and supported. Hashem tells us: בָּרָאתִי יֵצֶר הָרָע וּבָרָאתִי לוֹ תוֹרָה תַּבְלִין, *I created the Yetzer Hara, and I created the Torah as a spice to counteract it* (*Kiddushin* 30b). Rav Eliyahu Lopian explains, "Torah is compared to a spice. A small amount of spice can transform a large pot of food by adding a pleasant flavor. So, too, if we add even a small amount of Torah extract to our pot of life, we will make our lives pleasant."

Introduction

One good way to learn any art is to consult the experts. The expert we are interested in doesn't generally rank among professionals — but she certainly is one in my book. I'm talking about the person who always remains cheerful despite difficulties. Her credentials are admirable: she gives out wafers, cholent, and lollipops to all the neighbors' children; she listens attentively when you speak to her no matter what your age; she doesn't get nervous on the highway during rush hour; she maintains an open door to her home and heart, smiles consistently and converses with a cheerful voice.

These experts receive their training on the front lines, in any one of two-dozen "high-risk" locales, and their "ammunition" is unconventional. The battlefield may be in the kitchen, for example, where their eighteen-month-old son has just broken a dozen eggs on the freshly washed floor. Before running for a rag, the expert runs for a camera to capture his fascinated, innocent smile. The expert's strategy for combating chair-climbers is to tie the dining room chairs to each other and to the table legs. (I'll bet you've never thought of that one.) And when she visits relatives with young children, she politely steps over toys and other obstacles in the hallways, while she smiles and pretends they are not there.

These "professionals" are not superhuman. Even on an "easy" day, they may experience a torrent of conflicting emotions — excitement, doubt, hope, fear, joy, anger, weariness, irritation, satisfaction, and peace. And their on-the-job-training takes place alongside the other challenges of their lives: one may be dealing with loneliness, while another copes with raising a handicapped child; a third maintains a cheerful disposition despite a decade of back pain and three major surgeries. They have taken their best advice from a master trainer — Shlomo Hamelech, the wisest of all men, who said: *"Tov Erech Apaim MiGibor, Umoshel B'Rucho Milokeid Ir"* — "One who is slow to anger is better than a strong man, and one who rules over his own temperament (is better) than one who conquers a city."

Wherever I go, people continually express a yearning to know how to maintain a cheerful disposition despite life's challenges. All of the tips I have shared with them, both in my workshops and in my first book, *There Will Never Be Another You*, have come from the participants themselves.

That is also how this book came to be written. Malky, a woman who attended many of the workshops, mentioned her dream of owning a book that she could refer to whenever she felt "down," one that would provide her with great advice for any pressing problem at hand. I wanted to write that book, so I did what I always do when I begin a project: I conducted a survey in one of my groups. In this case, that group was the Tuesday morning *Tehillim* class in my home. I said to the women, "Okay, concentrate for a minute. What do you do when you are taking care of all the children at once, and you feel pressured?" They are already used to my "concentrate-for-a-minute" questions, which frequently spark interesting discussions. But something entirely different happened this time.

When I passed out index cards and asked everyone to write down their responses, I did not get the usual wholehearted flow of ideas. Some people said, "Well.... I don't know now, but as soon as I'm out the door and on the way home I'll have the perfect response." Others replied, "When you find out, be sure to tell me." Then I got a few impractical answers such as, "I get a babysitter/husband and go out for the night." I couldn't use the suggestions in a book that would be helpful to everyone.

Then I looked around the room and noticed that it was unusually quiet. No one had volunteered any additional comments or questions. With practice I had become fairly good at discerning the mood of a group, and although I now sensed clear discomfort among the women, I ignored these subtle hints. I really wanted this information, which I hoped would provide a fresh approach to a complex problem we all needed to solve. "After all," I told myself, "we are all in this predicament. If I knew how to remain free inside while surrounded by external pressures, life would be much pleasanter. Maybe if I put everyone's comments together, it would help us all."

Five minutes later someone looked at her watch and then at the front door. "Oh, my, it's 12:10. I didn't realize it was so late. I'd better get going," she exclaimed. Everyone else dropped the index cards on the table and exited with her. Why hadn't they lingered to hear their replies read aloud?

One card on the table said, "Don't read this aloud — it is for you. One has to realize that one may be putting others under stress by asking them to recollect moments of stress and what they did about it. I make an attempt to realize that everything — even stressful situations — is from Heaven."

It occurred to me that people feel pressured just thinking about stressful situations. They would rather talk in a positive vein.

So that is exactly the tactic I tried at the next workshop. Rather than asking about moments of stress, I asked about moments of confidence and hope, moments when the women felt they had received boosts of good cheer from Hashem and knew that He was right by their side. Their responses came easily and glowed with warmth, so numerous that I could barely record them all:

Sunset at the *Kosel*. Holding a newborn. A friend's smile. Meeting someone you admire. Flowers. Winning a traffic-ticket hearing. Putting up the Shabbos *blech* — early. Leaves changing color in the fall.

And that was only the beginning; the "good moments" seemed to build momentum. We thought of a young child screaming "*amain*" proudly, and a surprise cup of coffee brought to you by your third-grader. We mentioned baking *challah*, shopping for Shabbos, the inspiration of Yom Kippur, the delicate smell of the *esrog*; the joy of letters in the mailbox from Israel; the friend who called to talk when you felt lonely.

We thought of having surprise guests just when the house looks great; starting a new skirt for your daughter and finishing it; everyone liking everything you cooked for Shabbos; the appeal of messy braids on Shabbos morning; the family trip to visit cousins in Chicago; the magic smell of *besamim* at *havdalah*; buying yourself a candy bar. There were alumni classes and reunions, hundreds of men rushing to shul with their sons on Friday night, and the indescribable feeling of coming home and having everyone run to the door, joyously calling, "Mommy!"

Clearly we could have gone on and on. The atmosphere in the workshop was exuberant, completely different from the previous experience. People looked alert and eager, and everyone wanted to respond — even the woman who rarely spoke up because she felt self-conscious about her foreign accent. We sat together until 12:40, although the lecture normally ends at 12:00. People danced out, singing compliments: "This was such fun. Thank you! I know I want to come back. Your lecture made my day."

The women helped me to realize that the best antidotes to stress are the lovely daily occurrences that we need to savor consciously. It is up to us to put them on the map and make them into milestones. As my friend Goldie always says, "If you want to feel uplifted, it's not enough to notice the good in passing. You have to embellish the good." Embellish, according to Webster's, is "to endow with beauty and elegance by way of a notable addition." In this case, the "notable addition" refers to the conscious effort we must make to absorb good moments and pleasurable experiences, however small, into the routine of our daily lives.

In the end I did put together a list of these practical tips for a variety of everyday problems, and I'm grateful to my friends who showed me on that Tuesday morning a year ago that the best antidotes to stress are spiritual ones.

Let's pause here for a moment to address the objection that you don't have the spare moments to look for the good.

You probably do have particles of free time, but just aren't aware of them. It takes only a minute or two to work on your attitude. Everyone has to wait for someone or something a few times a day.

I call this free time "throwaway time." This refers to those intervals in your day when you are doing things that don't demand your complete attention, like waiting for the eggs to boil, doing dishes, or being placed on hold. Those moments don't have to go to waste; you can use them constructively by keeping your mind busy with good thoughts. Or you may want to treat yourself to a two-minute break several times a day, but instead of reaching for the phone, use the time to think.

Now, let's take a second pause while you object that a little bit of effort can't possibly make a difference.

Torah observance is accompanied by a supernatural guarantee: Our small effort is blessed and supported. Hashem says, בָּרָאתִי יֵצֶר הָרָע וּבָרָאתִי לוֹ תּוֹרָה תַּבְלִין , *I created the evil inclination and I created the Torah as a spice to counteract it* (*Kiddushin* 30b). Rav Eliyahu Lopian explains: "Torah is compared to a spice. A small amount of spice can add flavor to a large pot of food and make it more tasty. So too, if we add Torah extract to our "pot," we will make our lives pleasant and good."

When Goldie and I conclude our daily five minute learning session of *Gateway to Happiness*, she offers me this toast:

"Here's to happy thoughts!" Here is my offering to you of happy thoughts. May we merit to learn how to cope by using the Torah as our guide, and to create and enjoy pleasant and peaceful circumstances.

How to Use This Book

We are all busy. Each of us has a variety of responsibilities and obligations that eat up our time. Yet we all have a common need to nurture our inner selves, to nourish our hearts and minds.

This book offers you a variety of techniques that will help you minimize daily problems without requiring that you take a vacation from life.

The book is divided into three sections. The first section, "The Inner Voice," is designed to help you notice and understand your personal stress patterns. Before we can remove the barbs that annoy us, we have to know what and where they are.

Section two, "Learning," discusses the amazing treasures that lie easily within our reach, if we will only look for them. Tools for learning are all around us, some within the Torah itself and others within the people we know. Our Sages assert דֵעָה קָנִיתָ מַה חָסַרְתָּ, (*Nedarim* 41): one who has developed his mind has everything. The true king is the wise person. In these chapters you will find tips on developing not only a wise mind but a wise heart, and you will discover that learning can be an unpressured and joyful process.

The final section, "Daily Hassles," attacks the practical problems of daily life. In addition to concrete ideas for handling common frustrations like forgetting, you will find a game plan for the toughest times in your daily schedule. And along the way you will gain insight into the mystery of maintaining a cheerful attitude in every situation.

This is a workbook, and almost every chapter contains exercises and actual responses from the participants in my weekly workshops. The book will help you make lasting progress only if you take the time to do the exercises. Please don't skip them. Each chapter concludes with a page of practical tips to help you translate the ideas into your routine. For these practical hints, I've used only "kitchen-tested" recipes suggested by the "experts." All of the ideas have been applied successfully by myself and by the workshop participants.

Thank you for picking up this book. You have already taken the first step toward helping the sunshine break through the clouds in your life.

In Joy!

PART I:
THE INNER VOICE

Chapter 1
Taking Control

We are jolted out of bed early in the morning and sluggishly begin our routines. There are chores waiting to be done, deadlines frowning sternly at us and ambitions nagging for attention. People are pulling us in opposite directions and we have a headache even before we have left the house.

Unfortunately, we don't realize how often we sabotage ourselves. We make an unpleasant situation unworkable by telling ourselves, "I will be happier when my situation improves." We continually use the phrase "if only" in our inner dialogue : "If only I got more sleep at night; if only Esther would return my call; if only I lived somewhere else; if only my parents, brothers and sisters were more understanding; if only the Chanukah party were over (I should never have volunteered to help out) then I'd be happy."

Do you accept the premise that a miserable day will make

you feel miserable? How do you react if you've had a confrontation with a friend who let you down? If your car breaks down after it was at the mechanic yesterday ? If your instructor gave you a bad grade on a paper? If your boss confronted you with a difficult question? Do you accept with certainty that they have ruined your day?

In no place is it written that a miserable day is a foregone conclusion. If we accept that idea we have effectively relinquished control over our lives. We do not have to wait passively for circumstances to change in order to be happier. We can be happier right now by taking responsibility for *our attitudes and our spirituality*. Rebbetzin Esther Greenberg a"h used to say, "We think that if we change jobs or apartments we will be happy. However, we take ourselves wherever we go. Therefore, our happiness must grow from within."

I have fond memories of my weekly visits when I was in high school to my great-Aunt Rivka and Uncle Chaim. Aunt Rivka was one of those people who did not believe in a "miserable day." Her exceptional energy and zest for life were contagious. It was always spring when you were with her. She would look at you with interest and a sparkle of joy in her eye, and there was always one issue uppermost in her mind: "How can I give? What would make my husband, grandchild, relative, friend, really happy?" She never greeted you in a monotone, but always with a song in her voice, and her sense of humor helped people feel at home. Her clothes were calm and soft; she looked elegant, but not overpowering. Her ramrod straight posture reflected her attitude that life is a joy and not a burden.

I still remember the bright red umbrella she bought me for my fourth birthday. She explained, "I knew you really wanted an umbrella. I knew that your mother was worried that an umbrella could be dangerous. Look at this one. All the pointy ends are covered, so you won't hurt yourself when you push it open and close it. I'm so glad I found it for you." As I paraded up and down our steps with the umbrella, I was so happy, because it was exactly what I wanted.

When she was already very ill with the terminal disease that would eventually end her life, she flew to Toronto for her granddaughter's wedding. Not only that, but she danced at the wedding with the grace of a person half her age. After the wedding I complimented her: "Aunt Rivka, I think you are marvelous. You gave everyone who spoke to you your full attention. When you danced you looked regal." She smiled a little and then admitted to me that she had twisted her ankle on the way into the hall.

I remember a Sunday morning when I walked into Aunt Rivka's pleasant kitchen. It was a fairly large, sunny room with a sparkling black-and-white stove, a spotless white refrigerator, and two sinks. The small table was covered with a brightly embroidered tablecloth and set for two, with expensive china and silverware. The counters were completely clear. You could photograph this kitchen for a designer's portfolio on any ordinary weekday.

As I took off my coat, I commented, "Aunt Rivka, you are radiant this morning. The table is set for a party. Did anything special happen?"

My aunt responded, "Everything is the same as it was yesterday. Your uncle is still ill, and I still have dizzy spells. Today, however, I feel more optimistic about it, thank God. Let me share a story that my father[1] used to tell.

"There was a water carrier in the Baal Shem Tov's village. The Baal Shem Tov greeted him one evening and asked, 'How is everything?'

'Absolutely terrible,' the water carrier griped. 'I'm an old, weak man. This work is much too strenuous. I never get a chance to rest, and there is no one to help me. When I make an effort to climb stairs with these heavy buckets, the women complain that water spills on the steps. Life is miserable.'

"The Baal Shem Tov comforted the man and blessed him. A few weeks later he met the water carrier again and asked him, 'Have things improved?'

---

1. Rav Ben Zion Halberstam *zt"l*, who died in the Holocaust.

'Thank God,' the water carrier beamed. 'I am so fortunate. I may be old, but I am healthy and strong. I can afford basic necessities, and I need not burden my children. Not only am I independent, I can help others in my job. People depend on me; when I bring the water, they are grateful. Sometimes when I've climbed many steps on a cold day they serve me tea so that I have a chance to rest and warm up.' "

Aunt Rivka concluded, "The Baal Shem Tov explained that the water carrier's behavior was really not contradictory; Hashem had just given him the tools to make the most of his circumstances."

Sometimes our situation doesn't improve. We wake up to the same problems, the same limited resources, the same surroundings, and we spend our day involved in the same activities. However, we can choose to approach the day differently. Hashem would love to put a feeling of joy and hope in our hearts and if we only allowed it to enter, that slight change of attitude could alter our existence.

In *Mind as Healer, Mind as Slayer*, Kenneth R. Pelletier tells us that most standard medical textbooks attribute anywhere from 50 to 80 percent of all disease to psychosomatic or stress related origins. "Even the most conservative sources classify the following illnesses as psychosomatic: peptic ulcer, mucous colitis, ulcerative colitis, bronchial asthma, atopic dermatitis, hay fever, arthritis, hypertension, migraine headache, and sleep-onset insomnia."

This is quite an impressive list. Even more impressive is the fact that just as the mind can bring on such disorders, it can also get rid of them and supply us with enough joy to last a lifetime. The Vilna Gaon says that a person who has mastered being in a joyous state will be able to cure himself of disease; his joyous state will heal him. The *Orchos Tzaddikim* adds other benefits of a proper attitude: One's countenance glows, and he ages more slowly.

In this book we will review several life events and how you can handle them more effectively. In order to give you a feeling of growth as you proceed through the chapters, it is helpful to establish a baseline for your emotions. Exactly how "stressed-out" are you? Do you react to events with a high degree of tension? Everyone has moments when he or she would like to escape a situation completely — even Dovid HaMelech, who said, מִי יִתֶּן לִי אֵבֶר כַּיּוֹנָה, אָעוּפָה וְאֶשְׁכֹּנָה, "If only I had wings like a dove, I would fly far away and find rest" (*Tehillim* 55:7).

If you have that feeling sometimes, you are not alone, but it's helpful to know how severe your stress really is. Following is a stress questionnaire. Answer each question by writing a number that represents the intensity of your reaction, using the given key. (See the key below.) A low score signifies that you are exceptionally calm. A high score indicates that you should read on and learn the Torah skills that will enable you to not only cope with life, but to savor it.

Stress Questionnaire

Rating Scale: Answer each question below using the number of the response that most accurately reflects the frequency of each situation or feeling.

1. Never 2. Rarely 3. Sometimes 4. Frequently 5. All the time

1. I eat a healthy breakfast.	1	2	3	4	5
2. I have no pain in my joints or muscles.	1	2	3	4	5
3. I have cheerful thoughts.	1	2	3	4	5
4. I can concentrate when I read.	1	2	3	4	5
5. My teeth and jaws are comfortably relaxed.	1	2	3	4	5
6. When I have to wait for someone, I look for something constructive to do.	1	2	3	4	5
7. I enjoy meeting new people.	1	2	3	4	5
8. I function well even if the room is stuffy.	1	2	3	4	5
9. My heartbeat is steady and regular.	1	2	3	4	5

10. I feel a strong connection to my family.	1	2	3	4	5
11. I am able to be calm when others are inefficient or late to appointments.	1	2	3	4	5
12. I have no trouble asking for help when I need it.	1	2	3	4	5
13. I feel energetic at the beginning of the day.	1	2	3	4	5
14. I can handle my responsibilities even when I'm in pain.	1	2	3	4	5
15. When there is a lot to do, I plan ahead and make lists.	1	2	3	4	5
16. I push off dealing with issues.	1	2	3	4	5
17. I dwell on past mistakes.	1	2	3	4	5
18. My neck/back hurts in the morning.	1	2	3	4	5
19. I feel responsible to make difficult people happy/satisfied with me.	1	2	3	4	5
20. I scream.	1	2	3	4	5
21. I get dizzy and feel as if I can't walk.	1	2	3	4	5
22. I am too busy to sort out my thoughts and feelings.	1	2	3	4	5
23. I start but don't finish routine tasks.	1	2	3	4	5
24. I feel jealous of my friends and neighbors.	1	2	3	4	5
25. I misplace things.	1	2	3	4	5
26. I have trouble expressing my feelings.	1	2	3	4	5
27. I am not comfortable disagreeing with others.	1	2	3	4	5
28. I get tension headaches.	1	2	3	4	5
29. I panic when I go to the doctor or dentist.	1	2	3	4	5
30. I forget names, numbers, telephone messages, and what I am supposed to do next.	1	2	3	4	5

Total your responses to questions 1-15; then make a separate total for questions 16-30. Subtract the second number from the first.

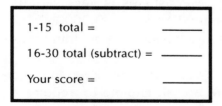

1-15 total =   _____

16-30 total (subtract) = _____

Your score =   _____

Evaluating Your Score

If you scored . . .

20 to 30

You are probably an inspiration to others! You have the ability to view difficult situations as challenges rather than obstacles. This book will give you an even deeper perception of the opportunities for joy that surround you.

10 to 20

Congratulations! You have learned to take your stress in stride. You will probably want to use this book as a reference for the specific aspects of your life that are difficult to handle.

0 to 10

Like most people, you are experiencing stress. Rather than knocking yourself for being unable to handle problems, take a positive stance. Congratulate yourself on your honesty about your feelings. When you complete the book, it will be encouraging to review your responses to the statements in the questionnaire and see how much you have grown.

If you are disappointed in your score, don't be discouraged. You can begin right away to remove the obstacles that are preventing you from leading a full and joyful life.

Yesterday I received a large brown envelope in the mail. I

opened it and read, "Suppose we told you, 'You were recently assigned the winning Superprize Number, but you didn't enter so we gave the $10,000,000 to someone else!'

"Deciding not to enter our Sweepstakes is very serious business. You could actually be holding $10,000,000 in your hand this very moment and lose it all because you didn't register your Prize Numbers."

As you begin your journey toward inner joy, keep in mind that every Jew is a finalist. We are all eligible to acquire a special prize that will guarantee that we will never again lack anything.

This is a unique spice with magical powers that is not on sale at the supermarket nor in any other store. It is available only in one place — inside you. It is the inner voice that speaks to you all day long. *Chazal* tell us — דֵעָה קָנִיתָ מַה חָסַרְתָּ, דֵעָה חָסַרְתָּ מַה קָנִיתָ (*Vayikra Rabba Aleph*, 6; *Tanchuma Vayikra Aleph*).

Your inner talk can change your whole life. If you are in the right frame of mind, you are a prizewinner. You need never lack for anything ever again in your life. If your inner voice is a negative one you are like the person who holds a winning ticket in his hand and never cashes it in.

At this point you may be thinking to yourself: "It's not so simple. Some people are naturally upbeat. They have a positive attitude without trying. I'm glad the water carrier could do it, but it's just not going to happen for me."

Don't fool yourself. Only a very small percentage of people are continually upbeat without expending much effort. The rest of us have to struggle. The good news is that the struggle is worth it, no matter what your natural temperament or pattern of behavior is. You can give yourself joy. The key is in retraining your inner voice.

A workshop participant once made a very insightful comment: "We do hear an inner voice at times that tries to reassure us and calm us down when we are angry. It's not a loud, harsh sound, like the trumpet that is usually blasting in our heads, reminding us about everything that is going wrong. This voice is a gentle, soothing sound. It's a voice from heaven

— soft and tranquil. I know I should listen, but I stubbornly ignore it."

In her final remark, this woman had pinpointed a very important truth: it is our choice to heed or ignore the positive voice that exists within every one of us. Why do we so often choose to ignore it?

> Sometimes the Yetzer Hora tries to persuade a person to commit a sin. He is not interested so much in the actual sin the person will do but in the depression that follows that sin. The depression and guilty feeling that follow the sin will cause more spiritual damage to the person than the actual sin itself. (<u>Cassette Series on Simcha,</u> Rabbi Shlomo Majeski)

"Does the *yetzer hora* really want us to be depressed? Why?" The answer is that sadness drains our energy. We can't do constructive things when we are down.

In the *Tanya*, our spiritual struggle is compared to a wrestling match. One man is much stronger than his adversary, but is sluggish and has no energy. His opponent quickly catches him off guard and overpowers him. When we are sad, the *yetzer hora* can easily overpower us, even though in reality we are stronger than him because Hashem is behind us.

The negative inner voice is primarily responsible for our sluggishness and lack of enthusiasm. Many of us tend to repeat negative thoughts to ourselves much more frequently than positive ones. We think that a really pleasant day, filled with good feelings, happens once a year. Actually, the opposite should be true. We don't need to slay a dragon to feel confident and content; we should be able to generate good feelings consistently through the small things that we do and the ordinary events that occur during the day.

You have just taken a stress test, but before reading on, it will be helpful to start off on the right foot. You may be surprised to discover that there are times when your positive voice actually wins. It has done so in the past — even once or twice — it can again. As one woman commented after taking the inventory: "Hey, maybe life isn't all that bad!"

Exercise: A Feelings Inventory

Rating Scale: Answer the questions below, indicating how often in the last week you remember experiencing each feeling.

0 — Rarely, or never felt / not at all in last week				
1 — Occasionally felt / once in last week				
2 — Felt often / twice in last week				
3 — Felt most of the time / three times in last week				
1. Energized	0	1	2	3
2. Calm	0	1	2	3
3. Hopeful	0	1	2	3
4. Relieved of a burden	0	1	2	3
5. No longer intimidated	0	1	2	3
6. Appreciated	0	1	2	3
7. Engrossed	0	1	2	3
8. Doubts dissolved	0	1	2	3
9. Happy for others	0	1	2	3
10. Confident	0	1	2	3
11. Comfortable	0	1	2	3
12. Proud	0	1	2	3
13. Strengthened	0	1	2	3
14. Talented	0	1	2	3
15. Courageous	0	1	2	3

Look over your inventory ratings. For any items which you gave a rating of 2 or 3, write a short description of the specific experience you had in mind when you answered the question. Keep in mind that in each instance, your inner voice was at work, choosing to give you a positive experience, whether you were fully conscious of it or not. The same voice could have persuaded you to ignore the good feeling or to find the worm in the rosebed. If you allowed a positive sensation to fill you once, you can do it again. You are in control.

_____

_____

_____

_____

A Feelings Inventory: True Responses

Energized — The children always make sure I'm not tired. The uproarious things they say can make you forget all fatigue. Last night they started dancing to the music on the tape and insisted I dance with them, when I felt I couldn't possibly move. My baby, who is not even walking yet, was standing and holding on to my chair. I couldn't resist her and within moments I was whirling around the room.

Calm — My phone was broken for one day. It was peaceful and quiet and I accomplished many things that had piled up on my list. Of course I was glad to have the phone fixed, but one quiet day was just what I needed.

Hopeful — I have a daughter who has difficulty going to sleep. She also wakes up at night and can be up for hours. I am taking her for sleep therapy and we are starting to see results. I am very hopeful even though it will be a long process.

Relieved of a Burden — I desperately needed a baby sitter for the same evening. I had made several calls and was starting to feel desperate. I felt as if a burden was lifted off my shoulders when a girl I trust agreed to come.

No Longer Intimidated — I used to feel intimidated by the cleaning help. Sometimes I even cleaned up before they came. Now I realize that I hire help to do a service and I don't have to impress them. So when a cleaning lady came this week to help in the house, she saw so many white shirts in the laundry that she asked, "Do you have a business here?" "No," I said, "these shirts all belong to my seven sons." I know I wouldn't have answered as openly a few months ago.

Proud — My daughter, who is not proficient in Yiddish, gave a talk in class in Yiddish and felt very good about herself. She made us proud as well.

Appreciated — Today a parent in my class gave me a Chanukah gift and a beautiful card. I felt encouraged by the nice things the mother wrote. My hard work as a teacher was appreciated.

Engrossed — I had just begun a new teaching job when I sprained my ankle. It really hurt, but I went in to teach anyway. I didn't want to miss work at the beginning of a new job. I found that being in class required so much concentration that I forgot about the pain in my ankle right up until the last bell, and then it returned.

Doubts Dissolved — I went to a specialist because I was having stomach pain. He advised an operation and gave a very discouraging report. Afterwards I went for a second opinion, and the second doctor said I didn't need the surgery right now — he could prescribe a special diet and specific medicines instead. I didn't know what to do. I was in a lot of pain. I went to Williamsburg to a particular Rebbe for a *brachah*. He said that he knew many people who used the second doctor and that I would have a complete recovery without surgery. I felt relieved, and all my doubts dissolved.

Happy for Others — I felt happy for my neighbor this week. She had rushed her child to the hospital on Shabbos. He had the Japanese flu which can be fatal if not detected in time. I saw them leaving and I was very concerned all day. I could think of nothing else. Thank God, her child is out of danger and recovering because he was treated in time. I am so relieved and happy for her.

Confident and Strengthened — When I got a fine for a ticket I had paid back in September I decided to go immediately and take care of the mistake. Although I hadn't been on a subway in a while, I kept my nerve and within two hours I was back home to pack to go out of town that evening. I saved $35.00 from the penalty and I was surprised at how fast I had done it.

Confident — At the check-out counter I said, "Thank you, children. It's great that you let Mommy shop today and cooperated in the store." The store owner said to me, "I hear mothers yelling many times, but I've never heard that before." That comment made me feel great and reminded me that I am doing many things right as a parent.

Comfortable — My two year old slept through the night for a whole week. I got a comfortable night's sleep.

Comfortable — My granddaughter had 104° temperature for three days in a row. I stayed up Saturday night to cook for her. I made a vegetable soup and baked fish. On Sunday I made her some vegetable juice. Then I brought all the food over and fed her. She felt so comfortable and I saw the color coming into her cheeks. She's only sixteen months old. She stretched out her arms and pulled me to her to give me a kiss. There was nothing as comfortable and lovely as that moment.

Hopeful — I know someone who is temporarily out of work. Last week I was able to find a volunteer job for her. I hope it will bring out her potential and lead to a new job for pay.

Strengthened — I was having a month of difficult mornings because of my pregnancy. I had no energy and felt almost nothing except dizziness. Last week I started asking Hashem for strength in my own words from the second I woke up. This has really helped me.

Talented — My sister's neighbor is renovating her house. She came and looked at how I've organized my closets. She was so excited about many of the ideas I use for saving space and keeping things neat. She insisted that I've done a better job than her interior decorator. I never realized I had a talent. The family joke is that I sat in the closet when I wanted peace and quiet from my four sisters so I'm good with closets. Maybe I could advertise a closet consulting service.

Courageous — Ever since I had surgery five years ago I stopped giving lectures because my memory was affected by a mistake in the anesthesia. Last week when I was on vacation someone who remembered that I was a teacher years ago asked if I would speak on Shabbos. She said they had no one else to speak. I was worried, but I decided that I would give it a try. It would only be for about fifteen women. I did it and it was quite nice. I'm glad I had the courage to say yes.

A Little Inner Joy Goes a Long Way

Practical Tips

1. Sit up straight. It will help you feel more awake. It will also help you feel taller which gives confidence.

2. Go out for some exercise, or at least for a walk. You will come back with a clear, refreshed mind.

3. You might find it beneficial to use your finger or other pointer. Your eyes naturally follow a moving object. It helps you focus your thoughts if your eyes have a guide to follow. Try this exercise: Use your finger to emphasize the tangible things around you that you enjoy — a picture, a letter, or an inspirational saying of our Sages. Pointing out something, even to yourself, emphasizes its value.

4. Post pictures of your loved ones having a good time in a notice-able place. Change the pictures every two weeks.

5. Put a sheet of paper up on your refrigerator for recording the little triumphs that happen each day in your family. (Optional- Use stationery or other decorative paper for this.) At the end of the week you have an instant letter to send to grandparents or an eld-erly relative living far away, or a perk list for yourself.

6. Smile, even if you don't feel like it. The effects are amazing. As Mashie said: "One day I decided to smile more often. My neigh-bor said, 'I think you lost weight. What diet are you on?' My mother said, 'Your *shaitel* looks nice today.' My children said, 'Mommy you look so pretty today.' Try it!"

Chapter 2
Demands on People

Part I: Demands on Ourselves

I f you were paying attention in the first chapter, you may have gotten the message that a great deal of stress is internally created. Stress is a choice; the difficulty very often begins with us.

Most of us are aware of the old and very accurate principle that the more we have, the more we want. However we tend to apply this idea only to material possessions. It is just as applicable to the expectations we have of ourselves. Most of us put pressure on ourselves at one time or another, and we never seem to feel satisfied with what we are able to accomplish. It feels as if we are on a roller coaster, going up and down several times a day. We frequently set unreasonable goals for ourselves, and then are disapppointed when we don't live up to our preconceived images of ourselves. Such thinking, however, limits our growth and development.

> Quite often a person's haphazard and negligent behavior stems from his <u>dissatisfaction with himself,</u> for when one is happy, he functions more efficiently; he fulfills his daily obligations in a more organized manner. When one is bothered he not only functions poorly, but even finds excuses to justify his behavior. (Focusing on Teshuva by Harav Chaim Pinchas Sheinberg, *Yated Neeman,* September 13, 1991)

Even when there is something that needs to be corrected, we should not flog ourselves in the process. Too often when we are working on a certain good trait, we decide that we want to be the ideal person right now. We want to be flawless in that area immediately. This is something we simply cannot have. Our eye sees the goal and desires it, but we just can't have the complete package right away, and when we expect it, we cause ourselves needless misery.

Acquiring a new trait is a long process and it takes a lot of practice. We should not be discouraged by partial failure in the initial stages, because that is part of the work involved in growth.

There are three common ways in which we trip ourselves up when working towards a goal:

1. When we realize that we must improve in one area, a single failure or error causes us to label ourselves pessimistically — and sometimes to give up entirely. If, for example, we misplace something, we stamp ourselves as unorganized. When we forget to give a telephone message, we call ourselves forgetful. If something we are cooking burns, we say we are "just not capable."

2. When something goes wrong, we use absolute words to

describe our lives, such as **always,, never, no one, or everyone.**
Since we can't always do the right thing, we are always doing
the wrong thing . . . However, such thinking is unrealistic. No
human being can always do the right thing all the time.

3. We allow our efforts to lapse, or even give up completely.
One mistake doesn't give us the right to stop trying. Steady
effort, no matter how slow or how minimal, yields the best
results in the long run. If you ate a candy bar today, don't give
up your diet altogether. Get back on track and keep going
without scolding yourself for the indulgence. Losing a pound
a week is better than nothing.

Negative behavior begins with our thoughts, and thoughts
are essentially statements that we make to ourselves. These
statements can cause as much anxiety as any external event.
When we make pressing statements to ourselves, we often
activate our autonomic nervous system, which prepares our
bodies to react to an emergency. Our hearts begin pounding,
the stomach churns, back muscles tense, and palms begin to
perspire. We get all worked up, yet we go nowhere.

If you think you are too demanding on yourself, try this
two-part exercise. It may be unpleasant at first to recall stressful situations, but acknowledging them is the first step toward
eliminating them.

Exercise: Get Off the Treadmill

1. Name a recent occasion when you felt extremely anxious.

_____

_____

2. What caused you to react so negatively ? (For example:
Did you want to make a good impression? Did you want someone you met to like you?)

_____

_____

_____

3. Can you pinpoint a pressing internal statement that you made to yourself? Complete one of the following sentences:

I should ————————————————————————————

I must ——————————————————————————————

I just can't stand it if I do not have ————————————

It will be awful if ——————————————————————

True Responses: Get Off the Treadmill

The women in the workshop took the treadmill test, and they were surprised to discover just how much pressure they were placing on themselves in each situation, even when their frustration was justified. See if you can identify with any of them.

1. I went shopping for a dress for my nephew's *bar mitzvah*. I had picked out a few dresses in my usual size, but when I went to try them on they were all too small.

Pressing statement: This is so embarrassing. I **should** diet. I **should** stop eating. I **should** exercise. I **should** be a size six.

2. I get very tense *Erev Shabbos*. I like to know what is in every drawer in the house at least on Friday.

Pressing statement: I **must** have the house in perfect order by Shabbos.

3. I was asked to speak in someone's home last week. As I walked in I noticed that the table was set as though for a *Sheva Brachos*, although it was a weekday. I wasn't prepared for such extravagance and was dressed too casually. I came at the time we agreed upon but had no seat. There were so many distractions; people were walking in and out. In the end I felt like a third wheel, totally inappropriate.

Pressing statement: I **have** to do this really well. I **must** make a good impression. The women **should** listen.

4. After the birth of my second baby, born 21 months after the first one, I was taking care of the children all day. I basically felt that was my most important job at that point.

Pressing statement: I **must** get the housework done. I'm not getting anywhere; I'm in jail at home.

5. My daughter wouldn't go to sleep on time. It was already eleven p.m. and she was still up. Imagine having to beg a two-year-old to go to sleep! I was so upset I made her cry.

Pressing statement: I **should** be a better parent. I **shouldn't** allow myself to fly off the handle so easily.

6. I was about fifty pounds overweight and visited an exercise salon in the hope of finally taking care of the problem once and for all. When my personal fitness instructor asked me, "What is your goal?" I pointed to a very slim woman who probably had a twenty inch waist. The instructor gulped and said hesitantly, "I guess it's possible — but you'll have to expect it to take twenty months, with three sessions a week for four hours each day."

Pressing statement: I **must** solve my problem quickly. I **must** be the perfect weight, or I can't face myself.

7. I'm in pain from a surgery I just had. I'm also not allowed to lift more than two pounds for several months. My house, which is usually neat, is starting to come apart. Whenever I see something out of place I feel as if someone has just punched me in the stomach.

Pressing statement: I'm tired of being sick already. My house **should** look like it always has.

8. We tried to buy my son a birthday present this Sunday. After walking all the way to Avenue M we found out that the store is closed every Sunday in the summer. I was so angry at myself.

Pressing statement: I **should** have called before I left. Now my son is angry and frustrated and it's my fault.

9. I couldn't sleep all night on Friday night because I had forgotten to order a huge *challah* for the *Sheva Brachos* I was making on Tuesday night.

Pressing statement: Every detail of the *Sheva Brachos* **must** be perfect. I'm not organized enough.

Part II: Demands on Others

The "pressing statements" that we make are not only directed at ourselves. The people around us bear the brunt of our internal labeling as well. It's problematic enough that we are harsh on ourselves, but we seldom have mercy when we feel others have not met their obligations.

I remember one particular incident in which I was surprised at how differently two people could react to the same situation, and it reminded me how important those internal voices are. I was waiting at the corner with my son, during the first week of school. Suddenly, the school bus came down the block and completely passed us without stopping.

I was very angry but this time I didn't keep my pressing statement to myself. I called the principal's wife and said, "The bus just passed me right by as I stood on the corner. It's not fair. I don't drive. The school should be more organized!"

The principal's wife said calmly, "My son is in nursery and his van hasn't come yet. Can you bring your son here and we will put him on the van? I'll tell them to wait." As I rushed up to her front door, a young woman carrying a baby in her arms welcomed me with a bright, gentle smile. "Are you Mrs. Schwarz? The van is waiting right there. Have a good day."

I thought about this wonderful woman on the way home. I had grumbled and criticized, but rather than labeling me a complainer, she repaid me with a radiant smile and went out of her way to wait for me. What inner statements had she made to herself that helped her react in such a peaceful manner? Surely they were different from mine!

As with self-judgment, tense reaction toward others begins in our heads. Are you critical of others? Even when you may be justifiably upset, do you tend to stew without doing anything constructive about it? The following exercise will help you acknowledge your internal judgments so that you can deal with them more effectively.

Exercise: When Others Fall Short

1. Name a recent occasion when someone did not meet his/her obligation toward you or did not "live up" to your expectations.

_____

_____

2. What caused you to react so negatively?

_____

_____

3. Can you pinpoint a pressing internal statement you made about the other person? Complete one of the following sentences:

He/she should _____

He/she must _____

I can't stand it if he/she doesn't _____

It will be awful if he/she _____

True Responses: When Others Fall Short

1. I feel upset when my husband's best friend, who isn't married, doesn't even acknowledge my presence. A short while ago, I tried to help him with a _shidduch_ and worked really hard on arranging the match, yet he never says hello to me when I am together with my husband.

Pressing statement: He **should** know better than to treat me like this. He has no manners.

2. I can't stand it when my son doesn't act with _derech eretz_.

Pressing statement: After all the training we give him at home he **should** behave better.

3. My husband seems to run out of the house just when I need help the most. Just when the baby is screaming he tells me it's time to go to *shul.*

Pressing statement: How **could** he run out and leave me to handle things alone? I do want him to go to *minyan* yet resent being left to handle things on my own.

4. I chaired a function for a school and had some girls take care of setting up. I was very upset when they gave me a $2,000.00 bill after the function.

Pressing statement: They had **no right** spending so much money without permission. They are irresponsible.

5. I have my friend's children for two weeks while she is in Israel. Her daughter does not clean up after herself at all. She leaves clutter and garbage all around the room.

Pressing statement: It annoys me. A twelve year old **should** make her bed and hang up her clothing.

6. If someone I know well does not greet me, I feel upset and think they are being snobbish.

Pressing statement: They **should** have manners.

7. I practice reading with my five year old. It takes her so long to read the word and she is constantly distracted, looking at everything in the room. After five minutes of this, I explode.

Pressing statement: She **should** try harder. She **should** at least look inside and pay attention. She knew the word yesterday and she should know it now.

8. I went to my friend's wedding and just as we were about to dance together she was called to another circle to dance with her aunts. She never did get to dance with me afterwards.

Pressing statement: She **should** have remembered to dance with me. I do a lot for her and we know each other for a long time.

9. Someone offered to help with "anything" I needed during the week of my daughter's wedding. I needed help setting up for Shabbos and she promised to come. I called twice on Friday morning, and each time she said, "I'll be over soon."

Pressing statement: She **should** have come on time. I shouldn't have to call twice and I'm not asking again.

10. I get annoyed when I'm trying to reach my friend and her answering machine is on.

Pressing statement: She **should** pick up the phone. I'm sure that she is home. She just isn't answering.

A Little Inner Joy Goes a Long Way

Practical Tips

1. Try to laugh or at least smile when something goes wrong. It defuses your tension immediately.

2. Learn to catch yourself in the act of making pressing statements. If you cannot squelch the statement altogether, at least modify its severity. Do not label yourself a "dummy" or an "incompetent." Instead tell yourself, "I made a mistake. Next time I'll do better."

Do not label other people either. We have a specific *mitzvah* in the Torah to give people the benefit of the doubt: בְּצֶדֶק תִּשְׁפֹּט עֲמִיתֶךָ, *Judge your friend graciously* (*Vayikra* 19:15). Rather than saying, "That person is conceited," tell yourself, "Perhaps that person has other concerns on his mind right now and doesn't realize the error in his behavior. When we next meet, things will go more smoothly."

3. Avoid the "absolute" words. Instead of saying, "I never get this recipe to come out right," try, "I seem to have trouble with this recipe. I'll call so-and-so for some tips and try again." Instead of saying, "No one ever helps me out," try, "People are busy with their own concerns and are doing their best. I'm sure I could get some help if I made a specific request."

4. Take action. Too often we make the mistake of assuming that people can read our minds. Instead of aggravating yourself with critical judgments, try approaching the other person with a specific suggestion that can alleviate the problem.

Chapter 3
Happiness:
Why Is It So Difficult?

"If a person insists on having everything he wishes, the lack of even a small pleasure can make him feel extremely unhappy. Excessive demands can even lead some people to consider their entire lives as worthless" (*Michtav M'Eliyahu*, vol. 1, p. 85).

When we learn to soften our demands on ourselves and on others, we are guaranteed to find a weight lifted from our shoulders. Our daily lives will ease considerably. There is one other area of demand which takes a heavy toll on us — our demands, conscious or unconscious, on God. It is here that the principle of "being satisfied with our lot" comes into play. Rabbi Yechezkel Levenstein tells us that no one is created with this trait. We all have to work on it and everyone learns it a different way.

The trait of appreciating the good that one has leads one to observe the Torah with relish and true awareness. Rabbeinu Bachya, the son of Pekuda, writes in *Chovos Halevavos* that this trait of appreciation leads to true fear of Heaven and a comprehensive love of Hashem. Furthermore, the service of one who has reached this level is truly beloved by God.

We must understand that one can only achieve this noble trait through thought and work. If one wants to become satisfied with his lot, he should specifically learn Torah thoughts and the book *Chovos Halevavos* (Duties of the Heart).

As we grow, however, we must not make the mistake of criticizing ourselves for our feelings.

> *A person should be aware that it is man's natural tendency to be selfish. It is a quality implanted in his nature, and one that can be overcome only with slow and painstaking effort. Every person is prone to this danger because his eyes convince him that he should want what he cannot have. This phenomenon has existed since the beginning of time, for the very first people that Hashem formed with His own hands were drawn after their eyes. They desired the fruit of the one tree that was forbidden to them and this was no more or less than human nature. (Ohr Yechezkel, Rav Yechezkel Levenstein, p. 19)*

Adam and Eve were not the only great people in the Scriptures to succumb to the allurements of their eyes. There are many examples in *Chumash* and *Navi* of the power of excessive desires.

When the Jewish nation miraculously conquered the city of Yericho in Israel, they promised that everything in it would be donated to the House of Hashem, the *mishkan* which was then in Shiloh. Yehoshua declared that it was forbidden for anyone to use any of the gold, silver, iron, or other precious items of Yericho for personal use. Any individual who took from the spoils of Yericho would jeopardize the entire Jewish nation. Yehoshua extended this warning to include the use of the land of Yericho, which would result in the death of the perpetrator's children. He swore, "Cursed be the man before Hashem who will build a house in Yericho. With the life of his eldest son he will set the foundation stone and with the life of his youngest he will complete the front door."

Achan was the wealthiest man in the tribe of Yehudah, the most prominent tribe in Israel (*Midrash Tanchuma, Massei*). Among the spoils of Yericho, he saw a beautiful cape that had been worn by the king of Bavel, as well as two hundred *shekalim* of silver and an intricately shaped piece of gold. They were so beautiful that temptation blinded him to the inevitable consequences of taking them.

Why did he think that he could get away with taking these spoils? The Sages give two reasons. The first is that Achan felt a certain superiority and immunity because of his lineage. He was from the tribe of Yehudah, while Yehoshua was only from the tribe of Ephraim. In those times, one's ancestry and roots meant a great deal more than they do to us today. Achan reasoned, "I am of the tribe from which kings will come. I am not afraid that Yehoshua will kill me, because my family and the members of my tribe will save me from him." The second reason he wasn't worried was because he had stolen before. He had taken sanctified booty three times in the days when Moshe Rabbeinu was alive and he thought that since he had not been punished then, he would not be punished now. However, he didn't realize that sins committed in private would only be punished publicly once the Jewish nation reached the holy soil of *Eretz Yisrael*.

Achan took several risks when he stole the booty of Yericho. He jeopardized the entire nation, and thirty-six people actually died as a result in the subsequent war against the city of Ai. He also risked his wealth and honor which he would lose if he were caught. Not only that, but the *Midrash Tanchuma* tells us that Achan only succeeded in taking the spoils without being seen because he stole them on Shabbos and hid them in his tent.

Logic would suggest that only an abnormal person would go to such extremes simply to obtain a few expensive items which he didn't really need. But Achan was not abnormal; he was simply human.

Once he saw the cape, all logical considerations became meaningless to him. In fact, his wealth and stature made him think he was invincible and he wasn't even afraid of desecrating the Shabbos. Achan's behavior demonstrates the reality of human nature: when one feels he absolutely must have a particular thing, this need overrides all other considerations.

Our first thought about Achan is that he was simply an evil greedy person and therefore his inner drive to acquire specifically that which he could not have doesn't apply to us. But Achan was not such a person. He regretted his sin and accepted upon himself the punishment of *sekilah*, stoning. His death earned him atonement for his sin. Achan is the author of the prayer עַל כֵּן נְקַוֶּה לְךָ. The first letters of its first three words — *Ayin, Caf, Nun* — spell out his name. We say this beautiful prayer every day, and on Rosh Hashanah and Yom Kippur, the holiest days of the year, it is part of the *Amidah* prayer.

When we recognize ourselves in these descriptions, we may feel concern and wonder what causes such excessive desires and how we can possibly control them. That's why it is important to remember that these tendencies are part of human nature, and that everyone struggles with them. We do not come into the world completely righteous. Good character traits and fear of Hashem have to be acquired. This type of learning never stops; it continues throughout life. What lessons about human nature does Achan's story teach us?

Achan's example shows us that wealth is not enough. There is always something one cannot have now that one will want. For that thing one will risk his life, his future and his present assets. Even if one can't use it, (Achan had to hide these items in his tent) he will want to possess it. The example of Alexander the Great shows even more absolutely that this craving never stops.

Alexander the Great was the emperor of Greece. He was responsible for the growth of Greek wisdom and culture and supported many scholars, philosophers, artists and athletes. He set out to conquer the world and introduce Greek enlightenment to all the lands of the earth and eventually his power extended over hundreds of thousands of people. Nothing could happen in the civilized world without his approval. Did he need anyone? Could any person living in his time period compete with him? Yet for him it was not enough.

The Midrash tells us (*Yalkut Me'am Loez, Bereishis*) that when he was exploring in Africa he once sat down to rest near a spring. The spring emitted a wonderful scent that he had never inhaled before, and when he tasted its waters he discovered that they had the magical power of restoring one's strength. Alexander followed the spring to its source and found himself at the entrance to the Garden of Eden. He raised his voice and ordered, "Open up the gates of the Garden of Eden and let me enter."

A heavenly voice answered him, "These gates are for those who fear God and only the righteous may enter."

"I am an important king, and I have conquered every city I reached," Alexander the Great argued.

The gates remained locked, and Alexander could not break through. After a while he made another attempt. "Can you please grant me at least one small request?" he entreated in a less demanding tone. "Since I have already reached this wonderful place, please give me some object, a memento, to prove that I reached the Garden of Eden."

Suddenly a hand came out of the gate and gave him a small round object.

When he returned to his palace, he decided to weigh the mysterious disc. It was light to carry, yet when he laid it on the scale, strange things happened. He placed a bar of gold on the opposite side of the balance but it was not heavy enough to tip the scale. He threw ten bars on the pan; the disc from the Garden of Eden did not lift. He threw a hundred, a thousand and finally all the gold he owned into the pan. No amount would outweigh the small round disc.

"This is impossible," Alexander thought. "What is happening here cannot be explained logically. " He called the Jewish sages and asked them, "Can you identify this object from the Garden of Eden and tell me why nothing I've put on the other weighing pan can make it rise?"

The sages explained, "If a person reaches the Garden of Eden, the object they will give him is something that can teach him a lesson he can apply to his life. You were given the eye of a human being. The nature of this eye is that it never knows satisfaction. It doesn't matter what its owner possesses; the eye always craves more.

"You have already conquered many countries, both near and far. If you will now stop going out to battle and focus instead on using the wealth you attained to improve your life and that of your citizens, you will live a long and fruitful life. If you continue, however, to go out and wage wars, you will eventually be killed in battle."

Alexander said, "Prove that your words are true."

The sages replied, "Take all the gold out of the other pan and cover the disc with some dust. You will find that afterwards even the smallest coin that you put on the opposite pan will tip the balance and cause the eye to rise."

Alexander did so and found that the words of the sages were accurate. He asked them the meaning. They replied, "The human eye is never satisfied as long as a person is alive, but once the soul leaves the earth and the body is covered with dust, it no longer has any use for wealth."

Alexander's story need not discourage us. Understanding our inborn needs and characteristics is the first step toward outgrowing them. As part of the process we will need to examine and perhaps dismantle some tendencies that society, our backgrounds and human nature have instilled in us.

What are we supposed to do? Examine the attitudes you hold dear. Some are hidden deeply in your psyche and you may have to ferret them out. Do you constantly aim for everything around you to be perfect? Do you wonder why things never measure up to your expectations? Who has given you the definition of "perfect" — your schoolmates? Fair-weather friends? The surrounding culture? Do you feel that unless your circumstances are "perfect," your life is not worthwhile?

There is a beautiful story that illustrates the futility of such craving:

> According to normal practice, Jewish men buy one esrog, one lulav, three hadassim and two aravos a few days before Succos each year. However, those who are really scrupulous about mitzvos buy more than one esrog, in the hope that if one of them is imperfect, another will be suitable for the mitzvah. A famous tzaddik in Poland was given two esrogim. One was an absolute beauty — the type one would expect to find in a picture book rather than in real life. It had every conceivable quality; it was spotless, well shaped, and had grooves all the way down the surface. The other esrog was acceptable but in no way outstanding, yet the Rebbe used it for the berachah on the first day of Yom Tov. His followers were bewildered but no one dared ask for an explanation.
>
> On Chol Hamoed an alarming discovery was made. The apparently flawless esrog was found to be a fake. The pittum, the fragile projection at the top, had been skillfully secured by means of a tiny pin, which invalidated the esrog for the mitzvah.
>
> The startled chassidim then asked the Rebbe how he had come to suspect the apparently flawless esrog. The Rebbe replied, "Perfection is a quality that does not exist in this world. To expect

it here is unreasonable; to imagine that you have it is foolish. That esrog gave an external impression of perfection — I became suspicious. I reckoned it would be safer to use the other one . . ."

If only we would appreciate what the Rebbe realized, we would be so much happier. At least fifty percent of our frustrations are self-imposed. Their origin is the misguided belief that we are entitled to expect perfection from our friends, the weather, our jobs, the government, and the bus service. The moment we come to terms with reality, settling for a fair compromise, we are holding the key to contentment. (In Search of Happiness, Pinchos Jung, p. 16)

It is not difficult to begin "settling for a fair compromise." If we just think for a moment, we will find much to be grateful for in our lives. Rav Yechezkel Levenstein tells us that it is most worthwhile to work on the trait of gratitude, because it is a foundation for both fear and love of Hashem. The key is to work on our thoughts and find Torah concepts that will help us change our focus. We can begin right now.

Exercise: Something I Have Right Now

Think of one time when you remember clearly feeling happy with what you have.

_____

_____

_____

_____

True Responses: Something I Have Right Now

1. I am a social worker. One of my clients just told me this story: "I was hospitalized two months ago. They removed a

tumor. I was weak and full of aches. I thought 'Why me? I'm only thirty years old.' Then someone else was brought into my room. She was just my age and she was undergoing further treatment because her tumor was malignant. I promise you, I stopped complaining. I realized I had to be grateful that I only went through a scare, but that the tumor was benign, and I'm going to be fine in a couple of weeks."

When I heard my client's story, I said to myself, "Well, I should be grateful I haven't been in the hospital this year at all!"

2. I feel as if I have wings when I leave work at four o'clock each day. Sometimes I feel I need a lot of things in the morning or late at night, but never at four o'clock. At four o'clock I feel like I have everything in the world. I work as a Psychiatric Nurse. At four o'clock I just walk out and close the door. I can go home and do whatever I want to do. These people can't leave the unit. Everyone thinks that crazy people are from Mars, but I work with these patients and many of them are from backgrounds similar to mine. Mental illness can hit anyone. So I just feel this great happiness that I can do for myself what other people can't do.

3. If I'm in a complaining mood, I think of someone who has something more serious to complain about. Then I call that person up and try to encourage her, and I forget my complaint.

4. I went to visit someone from our *shul* who is in the hospital. When I walked into that room I felt a tangible cheerfulness blow in with me, like a balloon. The woman couldn't speak but she opened her eyes and threw me a kiss. The fact that I can make such a difference trivialized all the little things I'm missing. They just were not important any more.

5. My mother called and told me about a really special kindness someone in our family had done for a neighbor. I thought to myself: "I have problems, but I also have people around me who care. My relatives are very special!" I felt much more cheerful.

6. I recently went to pay a *shivah* call to our Rav's family. They had lost their twenty-month-old son. It was so sad . . . At the same time, there were several stories in the news about parents leaving their small children all alone for days in a row. I had never appreciated having three very young, closely spaced kids as much before, but since then, I've really worked on maintaining this feeling. Because of it I feel my work load has gotten much easier — even though in reality it hasn't.

7. When I lost a girl child named for two grandmothers and had many other *tzoros* that same year, I went to a Rav for a *berachah*, and he blessed me that I should have a boy. My first feeling was one of disappointment, because I really wanted a girl. I had two miscarriages the next year, and both times was rushed to the hospital because of hemorrhaging. When I finally had a normal pregnancy and heard that it was a boy, I was ecstatic. I know that it's foolish to want a boy or a girl. A parent should just be thankful to have a healthy child, whatever gender it may be. I don't take having a healthy child for granted anymore.

8. My grandchild made me some little knickknacks. I hung them from my chandelier so that I will always remember her and feel grateful for such a beautiful granddaughter.

A Little Inner Joy Goes a Long Way

Practical Tips
Enjoying What You Have

1. Focus on five specific components of something you enjoy. Years ago I returned from a wagon ride in Prospect Park with my family and commented to my neighbor that I thought wagon rides were really lovely. My neighbor, who came from a small town in Hungary where the only mode of transportation sixty years ago was wagons, laughed and said, "On a sunny day like today wagons are lovely, but most of the time cars have many advantages." Now, whenever I can hop into a car in poor weather I think about that exchange and enjoy the factors that make a car comfortable and warm. I consider the roof of the car, the insulation, the heat, the speed at which I'm traveling, and the upholstered seats. There are many others but five is a good start.

2. Enjoy your progress while you are in the midst of a large task. When you clean a really messy room, make a list first of the areas that need work. As you cross off each item you have already accomplished give yourself thirty seconds to enjoy that corner of the room.

3. Turn on some pleasant music. It creates a background that enhances whatever you are doing.

4. Tell a child or a parent or a good friend about the little things you enjoy. It will double your joy.

5. A recent study asserts that there are two hundred and sixty different varieties of fruits and vegetables in the average supermarket. Employ all your senses to enjoy the different textures of food on your plate, the softness of the clothes you are wearing, and the variety of color in your life.

PART II: LEARNING

Chapter 4
Learning From
the Torah

After a particularly satisfying exchange of Torah thoughts with Nina, she said to me, "I'd like to ask you about something that has bothered me for a while."

I nodded and smiled.

Nina began, "My only experience with Torah learning was the year I spent in Neve Yerushalayim, in Israel. They had no routine tests at the seminary, but through class discussions, *Tanach* bees, and independent projects, they made sure that we were retaining the material.

"I was recently a guest at the home of a family. Their teenage daughter was studying all afternoon for a final exam in

Navi. She studied for it exactly as I would have studied for a history exam when I was in high school. I was surprised, because I had always thought that Torah subjects were taught in a totally different way from secular subjects. Is it wrong for me to expect that there should be a certain enthusiasm for Torah studies — a certain joyous attitude? Everything in this girl's approach seemed to indicate that she would rather be doing something else right now."

Nina's comment made me think. There was certainly truth to it. At what point along the way does our enthusiasm for learning evaporate? How can we find that spark again ? The Sages emphasize time and again that a Torah Jew can only achieve inner success if he finds joy in learning and practicing Torah. Wouldn't our lives change radically if we were able to incorporate that ideal?

Many women I've met feel that as busy wives and mothers, they just don't have time or patience to study Torah books. I strongly feel that learning shouldn't end when you graduate from school — but it may be helpful to understand that there are two kinds of learning. Let's call them "school-learning" and "life-learning." Each one is responsible for giving you certain skills, and both types of learning should ideally work together.

School-learning lays the foundation. It teaches you in a linear and logical manner the facts you need to know. In the study of Torah or *Navi,* for example, you memorize many details and learn the translations of the difficult words. At the end of the term you are responsible for organizing all the relevant facts you've learned, so that you have a comprehensive idea of Jewish history, laws, and Torah personalities.

Life-learning is random and intuitive. By "life-learning" I am not just referring to life experience, but to open discussion — a more informal but no less effective way to grow. Sometimes a teacher will tell a personal story to illustrate the relevance of a Torah lesson to our lives, or a free-flowing class discussion may take place, which can help individual students uncover their feelings and ideas. These occasions are rare, however, because of the pressure in school to cover textual ground. In fact, students smile when a teacher allows them to have a discussion, feeling that they triumphed and got her to "waste time"; and the teacher herself may feel embarrassed for getting carried away. Yet it is these stories and discussions that can actually help us to become better Jews, in a practical manner. Years after graduation, a student will remember only half a dozen verses of *Tehillim* that she learned in school — and these are most likely to be the ones that the teacher connected to her life through story and discussion.

In the classes and workshops that I give to adult women the scale is tipped toward life-learning. We do use a text, but at least half of each session is devoted to discussion and the sharing of experiences. These women have spent many years studying the secular experts on human nature, and now they want something more. We've been struggling to piece together a deeper understanding of ourselves based on Torah and the sayings of the Sages. We look for references in Torah books that can show us how to improve our lives.

The Search Never Ends

There is a passage in the Rambam's *Hilchos Teshuvah* that succinctly expresses the great need to attach ourselves to God through learning, and the great good that can be ours through the pursuit of such a lifestyle. When I hear it, I feel a spark of joy. The passage expresses our ideal life's goal and tells us how to reach it:

> It is proven and clear that love of Hashem will not be firmly entrenched in a person's heart unless he ponders it constantly and completely. He should disregard everything in the world besides this, as Hashem commanded us in Krias Shema: "With **all** your heart and **all** your soul." How does one acquire love of Hashem? Through knowledge of Hashem and His ways. The measure of one's love will depend on

his knowledge. If he knows only a little, it will be small, and if he knows a lot, his love will be great. Therefore, a person should devote himself to knowing and understanding all the wisdoms that reveal his Creator according to his comprehension and abilities (Hilchos Teshuvah, Rambam, *10:6).*

I had learned this paragraph ten years ago. I was sure of it when I found the *Hilchos Teshuvah* booklet under a pile of books in the basement, turned to the last page, and found some key words underlined in pencil. That pencil marking told me, "You have been here before." Yet I hadn't understood the passage when I learned it then, because it didn't connect to my life. I had been shown a beautiful picture, but my vision wasn't broad enough to understand it deeply. How much can one see when she is eighteen? Isn't it funny? If you had asked me then, I'd have said I knew it all.

The passage meant so little then except in theory, but today it is magic; and that is true in general of my experience in school. During those years I studied and learned, but I couldn't perceive a definite, strong connection between the words of the *Chumash* I was trying to translate and a surging feeling of love for Hashem. That learning experience was not wasted: it was the foundation for a later and more mature application of Torah principles to life.

When I was in seminary, one of our teachers once gave us a lesson that really drove home the value of learning. It was her second *Chumash* lesson, and she had given us a homework assignment. Each of us had spent two hours trying to find the answers to four of the eleven questions on the sheet, and we had all failed. The dorm was buzzing as eighty-three girls struggled to solve the riddle. Class the next day was enveloped in suspense. What were the answers to those four questions?

The teacher said to us, "I can't give you the answers to these questions. We haven't found them yet but we are looking. The term the Sages use is צָרִיךְ עִיּוּן — 'This needs further investigation.' Even though we don't have the answers, it is good to have the questions. It is a healthy realization to know that Torah is an endless search."

At that time I didn't understand what she meant. I shrugged my shoulders and thought, "I don't get it. Not fair! This woman has tricked me into two hours of hard work for no reason." Actually she had unveiled a beautiful picture to us, and even though I couldn't focus on it, the picture continually challenged me.

When I graduated, I continued to learn and teach Torah, and with time the learning has acquired a deeper dimension. Now I do understand the concept that learning leads to love of Hashem — because the learning I do now is my learning. I don't do it to get a teacher's degree or because I want a good grade. I learn because I love it, and that love becomes love of Hashem: an overwhelming excitement and a sweet joy.

I read a story about Rav Aharon Kotler, *zt"l* that is a great testimony to the joy of Torah learning.

Rav Aharon's Joy

One day a *talmid* at Beth Medrash Govoha passed by the office of Rav Aharon Kotler and saw the Rosh Yeshiva dancing — all alone! The *talmid* watched in amazement until Rav Aharon noticed him and asked him to summon one of the yeshiva's outstanding *talmidim* to the office.

Rav Aharon spoke privately with the second *talmid* for some time. Afterward, the first *talmid* approached the second, related what he had seen, and asked why Rav Aharon had summoned him.

The *bochur* replied, "For over twenty years, the Rosh Yeshiva has been trying to understand a comment of the *Gra* to *Choshen Mishpat*, chapter 28. Today, he finally arrived at what he is certain is the correct explanation. This is why the Rosh Yeshiva was dancing. He summoned me to relate the *p'shat* (explanation) that he had figured out." (*For Love of Torah*, R' Shimon Finkelman, p. 157)

The concept of צָרִיךְ עִיּוּן is both a testimony to the depth of Torah, and a gift to us, for we will reap the rewards of our searching — even if we never come up with the answer. When one cares enough about a question to search for the answer, it is proof of his faith, love, and dedication to Hashem.

Do you ever tire of looking at your grandchild's photograph? Imagine that pleasure multiplied a hundredfold. Imagine the gift of an endless search. Torah is forever; it is a pleasure that is never used up, a wisdom without end. Did you ever read a book and feel sad when you reached the last page because you knew the enjoyable experience was over? In the Torah there is never a last page. It is always there, and always refreshing and pertinent.

One of the healthiest things we can do for ourselves is to learn — even if it is only a small amount at a time, even if it is done informally. We feel happy when we learn Torah. There is a pleasure in learning Torah books and there is also a pleasure in learning to fulfill our responsibilities in serving Hashem. We feel pleasure when we learn a better way of doing something, whether it is adding to the joy of a Shabbos or a holiday with a new recipe, or finding out how to teach our children good character traits. When a mother begins to feel emotionally drained because her life has become an endless cycle of routine tasks, that is the best time to begin a learning project — even if it's something simple that only takes a few hours to master.

Learning can really change our focus and make us feel better — literally. This is because emotional energy affects us physically by setting off a complex process that starts in the cerebrum, the thinking part of the brain. The thoughts we have act on the hypothalamus, the part of the brain that regulates metabolic processes, the nervous system, and chemical balances in the body. Positive thoughts and the good feelings that result from them can literally make you stronger.

In this exercise, the participants described how spiritual insights helped them to feel that enchanting energy.

Exercise: Torah Concepts in Daily Life

Name a Torah concept you learned that left a special impact on you. Explain its practical significance and how it helped you feel better.

_____

_____

_____

_____

_____

True Responses: Torah Concepts in Daily Life

1. I'm having a very hard pregnancy. I keep wondering, "How do all these women manage their large families? I'm having such a difficult time physically, it's hard to feel spiritual about it."

On one of Rabbi Avigdor Miller's tapes someone asked, "We are supposed to follow Hashem's character traits in everything, as it says, וְהָלַכְתָּ בִּדְרָכָיו, *You shall walk in His ways.* What about Hashem's attribute of being a general at war? Are we supposed to fight?"

Rabbi Miller said, "Every parent who raises a family is raising a group of soldiers for Hashem. You know those mothers in Meah Shearim who have fourteen children? They are raising a platoon of servants for Hashem."

I've repeated this concept to myself many times, and it puts my life on a different level.

2. At a *Pirkei Avos* class the teacher spoke about the importance of giving people the benefit of the doubt. Two days later I went to look at an apartment that was for rent. It was in terrible shape; the ceramic tile was cracked, and the windows were broken. The landlord had no complaints, even though it was obvious that the former tenants had caused this damage.

He didn't berate the people or talk about them. All he said was that the family was returning overseas and that they had many health-related problems.

I've had several unexpected setbacks recently, but I resolved when I walked out of that apartment to accept them better and to try to think well of others.

3. On a Torah tape I heard Rabbi Yosefi speak about the great merit of teaching people Torah. He said, "In the *Chovos Halevavos,* Rabbeinu Bachya says that one who teaches others the ways of Hashem is greater than a prophet." I absolutely cannot do public speaking, so I wondered how I could perform this great deed. A week later someone told me about a tape library in the neighborhood. It turns out that the woman who organizes it is the very person with whom I've been waiting at the bus stop for my son to come home from school for two years already.

The next day I asked her, "Are you the one who has a tape library?" And I began borrowing tapes. I listened to 33 tapes in one month. Visiting this woman and seeing how she set the library up gave me the impetus to put my own vast collection of tapes together. I am also opening a tape library as a merit for my mother-in-law, who recently passed away. You never know how one suggestion will come full circle.

4. My grandfather is the chief rabbi of a Sefardic community in America. He is 95 years old. Last week he had minor surgery. When they brought him to his room, he had five tubes attached to him, but his face was pure and peaceful. He said, "thank you" to every nurse and doctor and all the other people who walked into the room.

Yesterday was his first day home, and I went to visit. "How are you?" I asked.

"I have pain, but nothing hurts me," he replied.

"This I don't understand," I replied. "How can it be that pain doesn't hurt?"

"Because I am too busy thinking about *Moshiach* to think about the pain," he said with a smile.

"Tell me about *Moshiach*, because I also want to feel so calm," I pleaded.

My grandfather told me to bring him a piece of paper. He took the paper and folded it up into a tiny, tiny square. "This is Yerushalayim now," he said. "But when *Moshiach* comes, all the Jews in the world will come to Yerushalayim, and it will grow — like this." He unfolded the creases one by one, each time naming a different group of Jews who will come to Yerushalayim. He slowly described the wonderful peace and the unity that will envelop the world as the paper expanded. "Each Jew will have his own palace, with hundreds of servants, and gold and silver will cover the streets . . . "

He is so full of vitality; he lives so nicely. He was up and about from the first minute he came home. He went to *shul*, and does everything for himself. I really feel that he will see *Moshiach*.

After that visit the entire picture I had of my life changed. I realized that I complain because I think only of my little world, like the paper when it was folded up so small. I have to think about the big, big paper that will unfold at the end. I am a Jewish daughter, Hashem's child, and I'm part of a larger plan.

5. I was visiting someone in Lakewood for Shabbos. Her husband has devoted his life to learning, and they have a very limited budget. I really admired her ability to take care of her family's many needs in an appealing way. On Shabbos morning, we were sitting on her old but comfortable living room couch, and I asked her how she makes ends meet.

"I have a special secret — I always prepare extra for Shabbos. Our Sages say (*Beitzah* 16): 'All of one's food expenses are fixed between Rosh Hashana and Yom Kippur except for the money he spends on Shabbos. If he spends less on Shabbos, he will have less; if he spends more, he will have more.' There were so many times when we didn't know how we would manage, and then Hashem sent us what we needed. I really feel that it is in the merit of Shabbos."

6. I once saw in the *Malbim* on *Mishlei* that the ordinary conversation of a *tzaddik* is a source of mental nourishment. Since then, whenever I read a biography of a Torah sage, I highlight inspiring paragraphs. This way, even if I'm in a hurry, I always have access to a quick "snack" of inspiring ideas.

7. In one of Rabbi Tauber's books he wrote about the fact that Hashem's ways are hidden from us. He said, "Success is not always what we perceive it to be in our own narrow-minded view. Sometimes what we think is our worst day is counted by Hashem as our greatest success." He wrote of an incident where he was delayed for three hours in the airport on his way to Atlanta for a Torah seminar. When he finally came to the seminar, he told his audience about the delay. He added that he had no idea why it had happened, but since God has a purpose for everything, he was secure in the knowledge that the delay was somehow part of the Divine plan. At the end of the weekend a fellow approached Rabbi Tauber and told him that the story about the airport had inspired him so much that he had decided to embrace religion. The Jewish concept that everything in the world is meaningful had deeply impressed him.

I read that page over three times in a row. At the time I had an illness that isn't so common. Although I am not fully recovered, the idea that everything is completely purposeful has given me the strength to handle the low times.

Chapter 5
Learning
From Others

Ben Zoma said, "Who is wise? One who learns from every person" (*Avos* 4:1).

The Rebbe of Zolotchov asks, "Why doesn't Ben Zomah say that the wise person learns from every teacher? Why does he say that he learns from every **person?** Ben Zoma's words signify that we are talking here not only about learning Torah from holy books, but about good attributes which can be learned from a person who excels in them. It is truly possible to learn something from everyone. Even if a person seems average but does one thing well, learn that one thing from him."

If we want to test this concept of "learning from everyone," we will find that we can go all the way back to the beginning — to infancy. Even a baby can be a model for positive behavior.

Rebbe Zusha of Anipoli said, "I have learned three things from an infant: His hands are always busy, so that he never sits without doing something; when he needs something, he cries immediately and asks for it persistently — he doesn't give up; and when his needs are met, he is always joyful, smiling and laughing."

We can continue to learn important traits from children as they grow older. One of the most prominent is their sheer love of learning, a quality which somehow fades in most us with the passage of time.

We are all born loving and seeking knowledge. Indeed, we all accomplished remarkable feats in our early years. We all started out knowing nothing, yet thanks to our youthful determination and curiosity, we succeeded. If we had only continued at that pace, we would all be brilliant by now. Think about it.

Children easily learn to do many things in their first years of life. Many children I know can speak at least three languages — English, Hebrew, and Yiddish for example. The European children I've met usually speak four or five languages. Young children learn to walk — no small accomplishment — and then how to ride a bicycle. They draw great pictures on paper (and on everything else), and they are marvelous climbers and jumpers. Close your eyes and take a deep breath whenever you watch a child jump off the monkey bars.

How do children learn? For one thing, they are gifted with natural curiosity — and the energy to pursue it. If it's very quiet in the room, you can assume your two-year-old is taking something apart. Kids want to touch everything and be everywhere, and we have to run around all day trying to keep up with them. They don't have the words "I can't" in their vocabulary. Try to explain to a three-year-old that his father's ten-speed bike is too big for him.

Another wonderful quality that children have is that they aren't ashamed to ask questions. For everything they see there is a "why?" or "what's this?" They are always asking us to draw pictures for them: "Mommy make me a car so I can make one."

Thirdly, kids have incredible powers of concentration. How many times have you had to say "Hurry up" to a six- or seven-year-old child? When there is something interesting happening, the entire world stops for him. If he is busy finding out how a calculator watch works, he no longer needs to get dressed, eat breakfast, or catch the school bus. There is nothing else on his mind besides that watch.

Children are great observers. Surely you have smiled at some point when you watched your child copy you. A little boy entangled in his father's *tallis* as he holds a *siddur* upside down and tries to pray with concentration is a beautiful sight. A child pushing a carriage and talking to her little dolls with the same words adults use, or directing traffic on his highway of building blocks, puts a smile on our faces.

These little ones are also very patient and determined. Once they decide, despite unsuccessful attempts, they will try again and again. A girl can jump rope for two hours every afternoon for weeks until she has mastered the art. She will draw the same picture repeatedly until she likes the results. She can make you wonder how many times a person can hit a ball with a paddle. I asked my daughter, "Weren't you scared to climb on a bike?" She answered, "I wanted to learn, more than I was scared. Everyone my age was doing it, and I wanted to be big, so I just had to learn."

Chavy began that fateful day on a two-wheeled bicycle thinking that she couldn't possibly go through with it. She did succeed, however, and her joy and sense of accomplishment were transferred directly into her attendance at day camp. She found that she could be just as successful overcoming shyness and making friends. This learning breakthrough led her to try other new activities — and her feeling of success eventually worked its way into the classroom. She decided that if she could ride a bike, make friends, learn new crafts, and get a prize in *shiur* for listening the best, she could succeed in mastering addition and subtraction as well.

Once we leave school, we seem to lose this momentum of our youth, and as a result we deprive ourselves of the happiness that comes with learning new skills. We become so busy just getting through the routine of the day that we don't have time for the luxury of "extra" learning. But the consequence is that we begin feeling haunted by a sense of inadequacy. As one mother said, "My mind is beginning to feel like oatmeal." Perhaps we just need to take a look at our own kids to get that dose of enthusiasm that we need.

Children are not the only people we can learn from. All around us there are friends, relatives, and acquaintances who have something to offer us.

On Ben Zomah's principle that the wise man is one who learns from others, the *Sefas Emes* comments: "At the very beginning of creation, Hashem planted in the human species this quality. Every person has something to teach others, **without exception.** The truly wise person has a talent for acquiring that 'special something' from every individual he meets. If one does not know how to learn from every person he meets, his wisdom hasn't yet matured."

Wherever we go we should actively seek information that can help us from anyone who is available. One person might have a fresh approach to a problem that has tied us down for a while; a second has an innovative supper menu that is delicious and easy to prepare; a third knows a creative way to braid *challah*. I have found that people love to talk about the things they do well and to offer advice. They will even call you and ask how your attempts worked out; and they will remember you through these encounters. Don't be surprised if many years from now someone stops you in the street and says, "Remember me? You came to see how I organized my closets five years ago."

Last summer in our bungalow colony it rained for four days in a row. By the fourth day we were all finding it difficult to maintain our sunny dispositions. One mother who specializes in decorating yarmulkas saved the day when she offered to host a workshop in the afternoon. Soon all the plans were in motion. Ten of us gave three dollars apiece to one mother who was going shopping in town. She came back with ten different fabric paints and a velvet *kippah* for each person. We met at two o'clock.

Many of us thought that we could never decorate a *kippah* because we had no drawing talent. Our "teacher" surprised us, however, with six or seven different choices of border patterns that even a beginner could do well. She also walked around helping us when we got stuck, drawing the first part of the pattern if need be, so that we could copy it and continue from there. A design that had once looked complicated when seen flying by on a five-year-old's head became a possibility when it was broken down into step-by-step instructions.

Two hours later all ten of us came out carrying a decorated *kippah*. We had gained a new skill, and we felt wonderful. I think it was the most enjoyable day of the summer.

This was not the first time that I had seen learning from others bear such marvelous fruit. The ability to learn a lasting skill from a friend had been given to me much earlier by a teacher I had in seminary named Mrs. Plitnik.

Mrs. Plitnik was a living legend. She did everything well. She taught fascinating lessons, cooked and baked professionally, and was involved in various philanthropic projects which kept her phone ringing constantly. When we went on a three-day tour to Eilat, Mrs. Plitnik was our chaperone. At that time she already had grandchildren, yet she climbed every mountain and crawled through every cave in the Sinai desert with us. There was one cave that had a particularly difficult passage near the mouth. About twenty students who had already come through it lined up with their cameras to take a picture of Mrs. Plitnik as she emerged. She was beaming. I didn't have a camera, but I took a picture in my mind of her glowing, friendly face, and that picture was never misplaced.

Once, on a Friday morning, we went to Mrs. Plitnik's house to learn how to bake *challah*. This was one of the things I could never imagine myself doing then. I just wasn't the domestic type. I had never once peeled an onion in all my high school years. Watching Mrs. Plitnik's quick, skillful movements was like watching an Olympic skier. I saw how she mixed the dough to a perfect consistency and braided it artfully, talking to us casually all the while. She was so good at it that she didn't need to concentrate. She told us: "I didn't always bake *challah*, but my husband said that *challah* is more important than cake. When I began, it tasted really heavy, but I persisted, and my family was patient until the recipe was perfected." I must admit candidly that I didn't believe any of this. Baking *challah* just seemed to be something that Mrs. Plitnik had been born to do. I couldn't believe she hadn't always done it well.

On that Friday morning, a seed was planted in me. I knew that someday, somewhere, I would try to emulate what I had seen. I would attempt to make that seed bear fruit.

About seven years later, after coming home from a seminar, I suddenly decided that I absolutely wanted to bake *challah*. I asked three different experts for their recipes and prayed for success, and the next morning I got up at six a.m. to get started. I had my doubts, but I took the plunge. I didn't worry about the outcome; I just decided to do my best. There was an overwhelming thirst in me to accomplish just this thing.

That first batch of *challah* was quite successful. As soon as I had taken it out of the oven, I called my mother to share the good news. She said, "Other people would have to spend $500 to find the satisfaction and excitement that I hear in your voice about this first batch of *challah*."

For the past three years we have eaten homemade *challah* every week. It has become part of my Shabbos preparations, like the fish or the chicken soup.

Remember the child's example, and don't be afraid to ask! Take advantage of every opportunity to exchange ideas and to swap skills. Your colleague might have a great packing list for a trip or for Pesach shopping, while you may have a no-fail method for decorating cakes. The possibilities are endless.

People not only learn mechanical skills from each other —

they can also learn how to live successfully. Support groups are an obvious example of assistance that is based on mutual exchange. Divorced women, people with handicaps, and parents of seriously ill children are only a few of the groups who learn much-needed coping skills from others who are experiencing, or have experienced, the same problem.

However, one does not have to have a serious problem, God forbid, in order to benefit from coping mechanisms for daily life. Fortunately, these opportunities are readily available if we are interested. After a lecture, for example, the fifteen-minute question-and-answer session can often prove more enjoyable and beneficial than the hour that preceded it.

I never anticipated that my own lectures would evolve into workshops on how to live. The small group and the homey atmosphere just seemed to make it happen. Each person's story gives the next person the courage to share ideas; it is a living example of the snowball effect. One woman who has been coming regularly for about two years once commented, "I've always wondered where you get so many different idealistic examples of healthy living to share with us. I thought about how lucky you are; you seem to know so many people with perfect character traits, so many model mothers and daughters who cope well with difficulties I dread just thinking about. I always used to wonder, 'How does Roiza know all these perfect people?'

"Last week at the lecture you told an anecdote that sounded vaguely familiar. I somehow felt I'd heard this story before. After the first few sentences, a sense of recognition hit me like a bolt of lightning. 'She's talking about me!' I realized. 'I'm the heroine in that story!' "

Each week real people learn from other real people. Everyone has something unique to teach and to give; no one is perfect, and everyone can benefit from someone else's original ideas. In the same way that other people swap recipes for *cholent*, we trade recipes for living better.

Workshops are not the only place to do this. All around us

are people who can help us — if we choose to make the effort. In fact, the most wonderful people to learn from are often those closest to us. Sometimes we find ourselves sitting and talking to a stranger for an hour, and we come away feeling very impressed; but in the meantime we've barely glanced at our own relatives and friends.

Rabbi Nachum Zeev Bornstein's son had been proposed as a match for the daughter of Rabbi Mendel of Kotzk, and Rabbi Mendel sent for the prospective father-in-law. "Is there anything new you can tell me about your son?" he asked.

"But my son is here!" Rabbi Nachum Zeev replied. "I'll call him and —"

"No, no," Rabbi Mendel interrupted, "you misunderstand me. I know all your son's qualities. What I wanted to know is whether *you* do!" (*Men of Distinction* p. 161).

Exercise: Learning From Others, Part I

Think of something — anything — that you picked up or learned, directly or indirectly, from someone else. Consciously acknowledging our benefactors not only increases our sense of gratitude to the people we know, it also gives us the reassuring feeling that help is available all around us.

1. I have learned that _____

_____

from _____
2. I have learned that _____

_____

from _____
3. I have learned that _____

_____

from _____

4. I have learned that _____

_____

from _____

True Responses: Learning From Others

1. **I have learned that** even a routine task can be meaningful if we have the right attitude when we do it **from** my mother-in-law. I happened to come over when she was ironing her husband's shirts, pressing each one with patience and love. She smiled as she worked, and when she folded the shirts, I saw how she caressed each fold and patted it gently into shape.

2. **I have learned** determination despite initial failure **from** my nine-year-old daughter. She decided to record a Purim tape for her grandparents in Florida. She must have pressed the wrong button, because after forty-five minutes of hard work she discovered that the tape was blank. She sighed but wasn't sad for long. She immediately started all over again, and her second tape came out even better than the first one would have.

3. **I have learned** to enjoy every milestone in my infant's development **from** a cousin who didn't have children for many years. She called me especially to share the news that her Yaakov now had two teeth, and that from the very first day they had come out, he had chewed with them.

4. **I have learned** the importance of sending a meal to a new mother **from** my friend. When my twins were two months old, she gave birth. The members of her shul called to offer her a week of meals. She told them to send the meals to me because she assumed that since I had twins, I could use the help even more. I had always been very efficient before the twins were born, but this time I was really having trouble coping. Those meals helped me pull through. Now I always send something cooked or baked to someone I know who has a newborn.

5. **I have learned** to write letters to my parents every week **from** Ruchoma Shain's book *Dearest Children*. She says in the introduction that she wrote to her parents every single week when they moved to *Eretz Yisrael*. Sometimes I've given up an hour or two of sleep to send out a letter, but I'm always glad I did.

6. **I have learned** how to handle pain **from** a friend and class-mate of mine who has a serious illness. She has two tumors that are inoperable. They cause constant pain, but there is nothing she can do about it medically. When she has spare time, she goes to sing for children in hospitals. When I asked her how she dealt with pain, she replied, "I read about how people survived the Holocaust, and despite the suffering, built up families and were active in community life." She had really internalized the message in the Holocaust books. The only thing I have ever heard her complain about is that her illness limits her ability to do things for others.

7. **I have learned** empathy **from** my neighbor. When I told her that my four-year-old daughter had a tooth extracted that day, I saw tears in her eyes. I think it's special when an adult cares that way about a child who is not even a relative.

8. **I have learned** to take a personal interest in people **from** my mother-in-law. Her husband was a doctor and she sent birthday cards to each of his patients for twenty years.

9. **I have learned** to plan important things in advance **from** my grandmother. Although I was only fourteen when she passed away, the beautiful needlepoint picture that she made for me as a wedding gift is proudly displayed in my dining room. She prepared a picture as a wedding gift for each grand-child way in advance; she rolled the pictures in tissue paper, stored them in a special drawer, and told my aunt to give them to us on our wedding days.

10. **I have learned** how to give advice **from** my neighbor, Olga Laker. When I had my first child, I decided that I wouldn't use baby food. However, I didn't know how to prepare regular meals for my infant, so I just fed her mashed-up table food.

My next-door neighbor had multiple sclerosis and couldn't move beyond her front porch. For weeks she planned a special surprise for me. She asked someone to purchase single-portion containers. Then she asked another to bring her the necessary groceries. Finally she called me and said," Can I borrow your food processor?"

When I came over, she had the supplies prepared and the chicken soup cooked. She then showed me how to grind the chicken and put it on one side of each container and grind the vegetables for the other side. "Now you can store it in the freezer; there are seven containers, so you have a meal for the baby for every day of the week," she said with a smile.

Exercise: Learning From Others, Part II

Make yourself aware of the qualities of someone close to you. Don't let the uniqueness of this individual become lost because there are too many things you have to take care of. Don't get so caught up in washing pots or doing laundry that you don't have a few minutes to look at your child or sit and talk with a friend.

Write down eight qualities of someone close to you. You can include skills that you admire.

1. _____

2. _____

3. _____

4. _____

5. _____

6. _____

7. _____

8. _____

What are two of the qualities that you would most like to emulate?

1. _____

2. _____

Don't stop at wishful thinking. Read ahead for a practical game plan that will help you not only to acquire good traits from this person but from others as well.

A Practical Plan of Action
You will need a calendar and notebook

1. On an inexpensive calendar reserved for your private use write one specific skill that you would like to acquire (life skill, mechanical skill, or otherwise) for each month of the year. You can plan ahead or take each month as it comes.

2. Divide a notebook into sections for each dream. Talk to people who have successfully accomplished each item and ask them for practical tips. When you notice an excerpt in a book that will help you, mark the place. As you accumulate ideas that would help you turn each idea into a reality, jot them in the appropriate sections of your notebook.

3. Decide beforehand that your first attempts will only be experiments, and that you will not expect perfect success immediately.

4. Do it! Each time you succeed, even on a small scale, treat yourself to something special and start dreaming up entries for next year's calendar.

PART III:
DAILY HASSLES

Chapter 6
The Benefit in
Every Situation

זְכָר דָּבָר לְעַבְדֶּךָ, עַל אֲשֶׁר יִחַלְתָּנִי זֹאת נֶחָמָתִי בְעָנְיִי, כִּי אִמְרָתְךָ
חִיָּתְנִי — *I will remember the promise You gave to Your servant and it will give me hope. I remember Your kindness and it comforts me in my suffering. Because Your promise refreshes me, I am no longer sad (Tehillim 119:49-50). (Translation based on the commentaries)*

D ovid Hamelech sang all his life, but his life was certainly no song. Dovid was constantly besieged with difficulties. He was ostracized as a child. His father-in-law, King Saul, pursued him. He fought many battles to ensure peace for the Jewish nation. Even in his old age, his own son Avshalom chased him from Jerusalem and threatened to kill him. Yet after all this David was still able to say in *Tehillim*, "I remember Your kindness, and it comforts me in my suffering."

> *We are told in the Talmud of another king who wished to sing songs of praise before God — none other than Nevuchadnezar, the Babylonian king who destroyed the Temple in Jerusalem and led the Jews into exile. When King Nevuchadnezar witnessed the miraculous salvation of Chananya, Mishael, and Azarya from the fiery inferno, he was so impressed that he was prepared to recite before God songs and praises of such grandeur and beauty as to put the entire Book of Psalms to shame. But an angel descended and struck him on the mouth (Sanhedrin 92b).*
>
> *An amazing story! How could this coarse, evil tyrant possibly outshine the brilliant eloquence of King David? And if indeed he could, why was he not permitted to do so?*
>
> *The Kotzker Rebbe answers: Of course, this heathen might well have composed poetry which surpassed the literary excellence of the Psalms; there are many degenerate, immoral writers who can boast of finely polished pens. However, literary style is not the hallmark of Tehillim. It's not so much what David said as when he said it.*
>
> *One can easily become ecstatic when experiencing good fortune. Anyone can rapturously extol God while he sits securely, watching miracles occur. But it is only the rare, unique individual who can continue to sing even when he falls, even after he is crushed and beaten. God sent an angel to test the sincerity of Nevuchadnezar's song: "Do you really wish to make sacred music? If so, then you will sing even after the blow!" (Overview/Artscroll Tehillim)*

The hallmark of a Jew is his ability to see the benefit in every situation, and to thank God for that benefit and trust in Him even in times of trouble.

I am reminded of a wonderful story about the Bluzhever Rebbe, Harav Yisroel Spira, zt"l, who was in Bergen Belsen, one of the most oppressive concentration camps of World War II. Once someone managed to get some margarine and with thread from his ragged clothes, the Rebbe improvised a Chanukah menorah. Many people came to see the Chanukah light and hear the blessings. The Rebbe recited the first blessing: "Thank You, Hashem, for commanding us to kindle the Chanukah lights." Then he recited the second blessing: "Thank You, Hashem, for performing miracles for our ancestors and for us." When he was about to recite the third blessing, he paused and turned his head. He saw a hundred eyes looking intently at him. Then he turned back and in a strong voice made the third blessing: "Thank You, Hashem, Who has kept us alive, sustained us, and brought us to this time."

A few minutes later someone approached the Rebbe and asked him, "I understand that you said the first two blessings, thanking Hashem for the commandments and for past miracles, but why did you say the third? Can we thank Hashem for keeping us alive and bringing us to this horrible place where we suffer, starve, and are butchered day after day?"

Rav Yisroel replied, "You are right. When I reached the third blessing, I had the same thought for a moment: 'Can I really thank Hashem for being here?' I turned my head to ask the distinguished rabbis who were standing near me what to do. When I saw a hundred eyes looking steadily at me, I was encouraged. Look at our holy nation! In the midst of the terrible suffering, they exhibit an awesome faith. They all endanger their lives to do this mitzvah. If I merited to see this wondrous greatness of my brothers, I must truly say the blessing, 'Thank You, Hashem, for keeping me alive, sustaining me and bringing me here.' "

Needless to say, we should never know of the terrible sufferings of the concentration camps of Europe. But the

Bluzhever Rebbe's story offers us an important approach to leading a healthy Jewish life. It is much more than the acceptance of suffering; it is the ability to put on different glasses, to lift ourselves out of the morass of negative thinking and find the silver lining in every situation.

Because we are human beings, this takes work. Our first reaction when we don't get what we expected is to complain. I once asked a friend of mine the secret of her optimism. She laughed and replied, "When I was about eight, I asked my father what optimism means. He told me about the cup being either half full or half empty. I walked away *positive* that my cup was half empty. You have to work on yourself, and little by little you change."

In *Gateway to Happiness*, Rabbi Zelig Pliskin gives us a profile of a man whose cup is always "half empty":

> *The story is told of a worker who always brought jelly sandwiches from home for lunch. A co-worker heard him mutter to himself, "Oh no, it's a jelly sandwich again. I hate jelly!" The co-worker asked, "Why don't you tell your wife to make you a different kind of sandwich?" "My wife doesn't make my sandwiches. I make them myself," was the reply. A person who makes himself miserable by repeating negative thoughts to himself is acting just as foolishly as this worker with his jelly sandwiches. He is needlessly making himself miserable.*
>
> *A person whose major focus is on what is wrong with himself or his environment or what might go wrong in the future is not thinking about the positive things of life. Such a person will be unhappy.*

One of my mother's favorite aphorisms is, "Be careful not to complain about something that is really a blessing, lest you be deprived of it, God forbid." We complain about so many things that are really good for us; about rain, about chores involved in raising children, about the stress of preparing for a family celebration, about the hundred and one daily hassles of running a Jewish home. We will be better Jews and improve our outlook if we are optimistic instead. Every time you stop to look for the favorable aspect of a situation, you enhance your feeling of well-being. After doing this many times, you will naturally look for the good. With time you'll be enjoying yourself more every day without even consciously thinking about it. You can't expect to handle every disappointment easily in the beginning. Perhaps at first you will have to grit your teeth, to smile and swallow a complaint, but if you stay with it, you will be amazed at your progress.

In the chapters that follow we will explore several things that we tend to gripe about: rain, waiting, and forgetting. The Torah outlook is that these are all actually sources of great benefit. We will also travel through your daily schedule and find ways to handle the various tensions of each part of the day.

Before we begin, let's stop for a moment and switch to a positive gear. The following exercise will help you discover that you really can see the ray of light behind the clouds — if you try.

Exercise: The Silver Lining

If we practice finding a bright spot in our minor disappointments, we will develop stronger coping mechanisms. Think of an unpleasant experience that you had recently. Did any good come out of it? Is there a way you could have looked at the situation differently in order to find the benefit?

_____

_____

_____

_____

_____

_____

True Responses: The Silver Lining

Here are some optimistic approaches to potentially upsetting situations from the women in the workshop. Some were able to maintain a positive outlook during the event; others report the beneficial outcome of a negative experience.

1. I was shopping at the grocery this morning. I took several jars of baby food and put them in my shopping cart. Suddenly, my child pulled out two jars and threw them on the floor. I was embarrassed and upset; I had to clean up as best as I could and pay for the damaged food. When I was picking up the pieces, I noticed that although they contained only fruit, these particular jars did not have any Kashrus certification. The other jars in my basket did have the kosher seal. I was so glad that I didn't wind up feeding my baby non-kosher food by mistake.

2. My oven was broken, and I couldn't bake. "Well, at least I can have a rest," I thought. "This week I'll let myself buy *challah* and cake from the bakery."

3. They didn't call me about a job as a substitute in the school where I usually work. You know, it's just as exciting to be home. I decided this would be my day. I'm going to straighten out my "junk" drawer so that I will be able to find all those little things when I need them.

4. I try to help out a particular family. The mother was assigned a specific date to renew her Food Coupons, but she couldn't make it. They said that they would hold a hearing to decide her case because she had missed the appointment. She really needed the extra financial help, and I was worried about her. It turned out at the hearing that they re-evaluated her case, and she got more coupons than she had received previously!

5. I was talking to my phone *chavrusa* (learning partner). She looked out her window and said wryly, "Look at that, they're digging up my street. They've been coming in repeatedly to shut off the water. I guess I have no water again. Today I'm on vacation — no washing, no cleaning!"

6. My husband admitted to the administrator of our son's yeshiva that we have a television, and the yeshiva threw us out, even though the television is in a box in the basement and the children rarely watch it. I resented this because I have had my older son in that school for ten years, and they know our family. They know we have strong principles. Although the change was forced on us, it turned out in our favor. Last year was a totally wasted year for the kids in the old yeshiva. In the new school my eight-year-old son is doing much better, and my six-year-old is a thousand times happier because they are in smaller classes. It was Hashem watching over us. Had I left them in the other school, they would have stagnated. Life is a very large picture, and we don't see all of it. We have to remember that Hashem is our Father Who cares about us. We have to start looking at things differently.

7. I go to work each day as a teacher in a public school. It's a strenuous occupation, but I try to look at all the "pluses." Besides the excellent benefits, I'm glad that I am in a financial position, *Boruch Hashem*, to pay full tuition for my son in yeshiva, so that someone else can have the benefit of a scholarship. Because I teach, my husband doesn't have to take on a second job. Lastly, I incorporate many moral values into my class lessons.

8. I was called to help set up for a charity function. We started out with six or seven women, but everyone found an excuse to leave early. At last I was stranded with just one other person. I was glad I was there though; no matter what situation I'm in, I try to learn something.

My partner in this kind act was a simple and very special woman, and the conversation was a pleasure. We talked about things of substance. She explained that in France when she was growing up, *Rosh Chodesh* was really a holiday. Her mother prepared special foods, the family all washed for bread and had chicken soup and *kneidlach*, and no one dared sew or wash. I was so glad I had met this woman. Maybe next month I'll at least remember to prepare a treat for *Rosh Chodesh*.

9. I get deliveries from two food stores on Thursday nights, and make up packages for needy families. There is never as much food as we would like to give. As we pick up each item to decide which family it should go to, we ask ourselves: "Who has a larger family? Who is out of work? Who is in *kollel?* Who is working but needs help?" Occasionally, despite our precise calculations, we deliver things by mistake to the wrong families. We tried writing down the names on removable labels, but there were still mistakes. I once wanted to deliver to an extra family that week because I had six boxes. It turned out I had only five boxes.

Finally, I decided that there are no mistakes. Hashem is deciding who gets each box, and He knows who needs it. Since then I feel aglow when I get into the van. I am a messenger from Hashem, and He picks up where we leave off. I believe I have *emunah*, but it helps when I see *hashgacha* (Divine Providence) in a tangible way.

Chapter 7
Waiting

In one of the workshops, Shayna said, "I get nervous when I have to go somewhere with my husband and he is late. The last time it was only fifteen minutes, and he did have a good reason but I sat and counted all the things he was doing now that he could have done earlier."

There are not too many people in the world who enjoy waiting. Even when we patiently wait, we are forced to quell our inborn energy. Mothers are forced to do quite a bit of waiting during the course of our otherwise busy days. We wait for the school bus several times a day; we wait for our husbands while we keep supper warm; we wait for our children to finish eating, put on pajamas, and fall asleep. We even wait for a five-year-old to figure out how to read the next word in the book while thinking that if he paid attention or tried harder, it wouldn't take him so long.

Although waiting is frustrating, it is essential that our need for efficiency not cause others emotional pain. When we pressure people to "hurry up," it creates stress both for them and for us. Last year I was asked to give a lecture outlining eight things you can do for your children every day. I decided to go straight to the source and solicit ideas from my eight-year-old daughter. When I asked her what she would like me to do for her, the first thing she said was, "Mommy, when we are walking and I feel a stone in my shoe, can you wait for me to shake it out?" Apparently my impatience had filtered through to her somewhere along the line.

Children are among the most important people we need to wait for. Have you ever noticed a child running along next to an adult? Sometimes they fall over their feet in an effort to keep up. Their anxious faces cry out, "Mommy, don't rush me. My legs can only take small steps. I'm not grown up. You are so smart and neat, and you know how to do everything. I feel so dumb."

Sara Lea reported a comment her four-year-old son had made that really hit home: "Mommy, when *you* want something, you say 'hurry up.' When *I* want something, you say 'wait'."

Goldie, an excellent kindergarten teacher, told me what she does to avoid saying "hurry up": "When we walk down the steps for recess, I say, 'Let's see who can take big steps like a Mommy.' I also composed a little song for the children about putting on coats and standing in a straight line. It helps the time pass pleasantly, and the kids don't feel hassled."

Waiting for children has its precedent in *Chumash*. In *Parashas Vayishlach*, we learn that Yaakov Avinu was careful to walk at his children's pace: *"And Yaakov said to Esav, 'My master knows that the children are young . . . May my master please go before his servant, and I will go slowly at the pace of my children's stride, until I meet you in Seir.'"* (*Bereishis* 33:14)

Of course, children are not the only people we must wait for. But it may help us to wait with less tension if we keep in mind that waiting is an act of kindness. When we go outside to wait for someone who is coming home, or stand at the door and wave goodbye to someone who is leaving, we show the person that he or she is precious to us. Last year, for our children's school yearbook, they interviewed the little boys in the kindergarten. They asked, "What does your mother do while you are in school?" The boys answered:

"My mother goes to work."

"My mother does the laundry."

"My mother cooks supper."

One little boy said, "My mother sits at the window and waits for me to come home." How lucky he is to feel secure in the belief that his mother sits all day and waits for him to come home!

Waiting for someone who is in distress can be a tremendous source of emotional support. If you have ever twiddled you thumbs in a doctor's office waiting for a relative to finish the examination, just think about what is going through the patient's mind. Very few doctor's visits are pleasant, and it is a wonderful comfort to know that someone is sitting out in the waiting room, ready to accompany us home.

I heard a heartwarming story recently from Miri, who welcomed her friend Chana from Israel. Chana had come to America for surgery, and Miri not only hosted her but also helped to raise money for medical expenses. Miri's story was not about herself, however; it was about a few other women who had performed the important *mitzvah* of waiting.

"You've heard of Mrs. L. from the *Neshei*," Miri told me. "This morning she was here at six a.m. to take Chana to the hospital for surgery. She hugged Chana as though she were her own daughter and encouraged her, 'Don't worry, the operation will go well, and you'll be healthy soon. You know, I used to be your size. I'm giving you all my dresses. I have lots of really nice things for you.' She stayed at the hospital and *waited* for her to come out of surgery. It took longer than expected and Mrs. L. had to leave at eleven o'clock, but my sister-in-law Chaya took over. She is there now, waiting for

Chana to come out. Chana should be able to leave by four o'clock this afternoon, and my other sister-in-law, Shaina, will pick her up and bring her home. Remember, these are all people who have never even met Chana!"

It is hardly necessary to describe what Chana herself must have felt, knowing that so many women put aside their own schedules just to wait for her and attend to her needs.

Of course, you don't have to be sick, God forbid, to appreciate the feeling of being waited for. If you have ever been on an airplane flight or a long bus ride, you know how relieved you are when you walk out of the gate and see a familiar person smiling and waving. Traveling drains both one's physical and emotional energy, especially if you are going to a strange country and know that you will not relax until you get there safely. Etty said, "We flew to Israel to visit our daughter, who was studying in a seminary in Yerushalayim. As we got into the airport, we spotted her behind the glass window waving a giant *Bruchim Habaim* welcome sign. It was such a good feeling to see her waiting for us after the long flight."

There are several wonderful examples in the Torah of people who were praised for waiting. One of these was Aharon the High Priest.

Moshe Rabbeinu, Aharon's brother, had been forced to leave Egypt because Pharaoh had attempted to execute him, and Aharon had tended the Jews for many years, in his place, listening to their troubles and keeping their hope alive prophetically. When Hashem commanded Moshe to return to Egypt and lead the Jews out of slavery, he was very reluctant to do so. He said, "Hashem, send the messenger that you have always sent until now. How can I take Aharon's position?" Hashem replied, "Don't worry, because Aharon will not be upset. Look, he is coming out to welcome you. When he sees you, he will be happy for you in his heart."

Aharon waited for Moshe on the road and encouraged him with his smiling countenance. *Rashi* tells us that Aharon's reward for rejoicing in his brother's honor was that he would wear the *Urim V'Tumim*, the breastplate that was consulted for Divine answers to the Jewish nation's questions. Aharon not only waited for his brother, but he waited with a joyous heart.

Miriam the prophetess, sister of Moshe and Aharon, is also credited with waiting. The Torah describes her standing from afar and watching over her infant brother, Moshe, who had been placed in a basket by the river in order to escape Pharaoh's decree of death against Jewish male children. Miriam waited for about fifteen minutes before Pharaoh's daughter came and saved her brother.

The *Yalkut Shimoni* quotes the Sages: "In the way that a person conducts himself, God responds towards him. Miriam waited for her brother for a short while, and in return, God made the Holy Ark and the *Shechinah*, the Priests and the Levites, the seven Clouds of Glory and the entire Jewish nation wait for Miriam." This refers to the time when Miriam was ill with *tzora'as*, leprosy, and the entire camp of Israel delayed their travels for a full week until she was cured.

Sanctified Time

Waiting is not only a *mitzvah* in itself. What we do with the time is important too. It doesn't have to go to waste. In fact, waiting-time can become sanctified time.

Once Rabbi Yitzchok of Vorke and his chassidim had to wait a very long time to recite *Kiddush Halevanah*, the blessing on the new moon. The moon was covered by clouds, and they could not recite the prayer. When his followers became impatient, the Rebbe said to them, "We have learned that a *mitzvah* draws along another *mitzvah* in its path. This teaches us that if the *mitzvah* literally drags out and one has to wait a long time to fulfill it, he should not get aggravated, because the time that he spends waiting and preparing is also a *mitzvah*. You will be rewarded for your waiting-time."

There is a wonderful story from Ruchoma Shain's *All for the Boss* that illustrates the reward of waiting-time well-spent.

One day, as Rabbi Mordechai Yoffe was walking along Norfolk Street on the East Side, he met Pappa. Pappa realized that Mordechai was very discouraged because all his attempts to meet the "right girl" seemed to be headed in the wrong direction.

Pappa grasped his hand as they walked together and said to him, "Reb Mordche, let me tell you a story. There was a rich Jew in Warsaw, Poland, who had a very profitable business. When he passed on, his son inherited the business. Though the son followed the same procedures as his father, he met with no success. After a period of time, the business was close to failure.

"It was then that the son sought the advice of the rebbe. He confided to the rebbe his deep concern about the deterioration of the business. The rebbe listened carefully to the son's discouraging tale and asked him, 'Tell me, what did your father do when there were no customers in the store?'

"The son answered, 'Whenever my father had a moment to spare, he engrossed himself in Torah learning or recited Tehillim.'

" 'And what do you do when the store is empty?' the rebbe questioned the son.

" 'I am not like my father. I read a newspaper or talk to a neighbor.'

" 'Now I have the answer to give you,' said the rebbe. 'When Satan saw your father busy learning Torah or reciting Tehillim, he was troubled. He therefore sent many customers to make sure that your father should not occupy himself with Torah studies. Of course, the business flourished. In your case, Satan is quite content when no customers appear, as you are busy with mundane activities.' "

Pappa finished his story and said to Reb Mordche, "You are also pleasing Satan. He notices that you cannot concentrate on your Torah studies and keeps you occupied trying to find your zivug, but he does all in his power not to allow her to reach you. Start your Torah learning in earnest, and Satan will see to it that your partner will put in her appearance very quickly."

Reb Mordche heeded Pappa's advice and once again became dedicated to his Torah studies. Not long after that he met his wife, Channah. Reb Mordche said to me, "I followed your father's excellent advice through different phases of my life, and it always proved to be correct."

Rabbi Mordechai Yoffe is the Rosh Yeshiva of Bais Torah in Monsey, New York.

Waiting time, as you can see, can be turned instantly from a burden into an opportunity. It is a *mitzvah*, a kindness, a space to be filled with positive activity. It may even be a blessing in disguise. When we give it, let's do so with patience and joy. We will be richly rewarded for our waiting-time. The following excerpt shows us that learning how to wait patiently is an integral element of spiritual maturity as well:

> *Jewish consciousness is that we say to a person, "Wait a bit." The yetzer hara says: "Feed me quickly, immediately, right now." The yetzer tov says, "Be still and wait a little. This thing you want will come to you by itself even if you wait a little, and perhaps if you wait a little you will be served more than you expected." (Imrei Noam, Rebbe of Valbarz; Nesivos Haosher)*

Exercise: Positive Waiting

When was the last time you had to wait a substantial

amount of time? What were the thoughts that were running through your head?

_____

_____

_____

_____

_____

If your thoughts were not very pleasant, don't despair. There *is* something you can do about it! While waiting, count your blessings. Think of ten pleasant things: experiences you have had, things you own, activities you enjoy. Keep this list posted in a place where you can refer to it while you wait, or carry it in your purse. You can always keep adding to the list.

1. _____

2. _____

3. _____

4. _____

5. _____

6. _____

7. _____

8. _____

9. _____

10. _____

A Little Inner Joy Goes a Long Way

Practical Tips for Waiting

1. Keep reading materials with you to enjoy while you wait for appointments or stand in lines. A walkman with Torah tapes is another good idea.

2. Don't come late. Allow ample time between appointments that you schedule so that you will not keep others waiting.

3. Clarify. Repeat directions and times, and repeat the other person's directions. Taking a minute to be sure you understand and are understood can save hours.

4. Be prepared with a contingency plan, and discuss the plans clearly: "If either of us is delayed or if we get separated in the supermarket, here's what we'll do . . . "

5. Perhaps your schedule is too congested. Write down five things in your daily schedule that require waiting, and the estimated time. Then add up the minutes. If this is more time than you can afford to spend during the day, consider dropping something from your routine.

6. Try to transform waiting time into an elevating experience.

Chapter 8
Forgetting

"**W**hen I forget something, I think very poorly of myself. The inconvenience isn't as bad as the feelings I have about it. I feel embarrassed and unsettled when I don't know where things are."

"Accomplishing is important to me. When something is missing, I panic and walk around aimlessly. The word WASTE looms big: a WASTE of time, a WASTE of energy. I tell myself I should be more careful. Sometimes I even get dizzy."

"As a child, if I forgot my homework at home, or even if my mother hadn't signed my homework pad, I was put in the corner. Today's teachers are still scolding my children for forgetting."

Do these remarks sound familiar? Do you feel out of control

when you are forgetful? Do you feel so overloaded that you forget to take care of things until the last minute? Do you hesitate to tell people you will return their phone calls — because you know you will forget?

There are many people who feel frustrated by their forgetfulness, so you are not alone. You may be relieved to know that forgetting has less to do with your mental ability than with your state of mind. If you have too many things to do, for example, you are likely to get confused. Uncluttering your schedule can also help you unclutter your head.

Forgetting can also be a defense mechanism. If there is something we want to avoid, we often say we will attend to it later — and then conveniently forget about it.

One major cause of forgetfulness is anger. Several women in my workshops have testified to the fact that "exploding" can weaken your memory. They are backed up by our Sages, who say, "If one who is wise becomes angry, his wisdom leaves him." (*Pesachim* 66:2)

We learn this principle from Moshe Rabbeinu. When Moshe became angry with the Jewish military leaders after the war with Midian (*Bamidbar* 31:14), he forgot the laws of *tevilas keilim* (immersing a vessel that had belonged to a gentile in a *mikvah*). Elazar, Aharon's son, stood up and declared these laws in his stead.

When the people left over *manna*, the food given to them in the desert, against Hashem's command and it became spoiled, Moshe became angry, and again, he forgot to tell the Jews something important. When they came home on Friday afternoon, they saw that their portion of *manna* had miraculously doubled. When Moshe saw this double portion he realized he had forgotten to tell them that on Friday they would receive extra *manna* so that they should not gather on Shabbos.

Was Moshe's anger in these cases justified? Clearly it was. The war against Midian was fought because the Jews had been lured into sin with the Midianite daughters. Moshe was angered when the Jewish soldiers took the female Midianites prisoner, thereby bringing the stumbling block into their camp. In the case of the *manna*, Hashem had made a tremendous miracle and given the Jews food from Heaven on the condition that they should not leave any over for the next day. Nevertheless, they rebelled against Hashem's command and did indeed save food from day to day. Moshe had good reasons for being angry with the Jews.

Despite the fact that the anger was justified, Moshe forgot. We learn from this that forgetting when one is angry isn't a punishment but a natural phenomenon. Anger burns up one's wisdom and causes it to be consumed.

Forgetting should also not be considered a serious fault, a concept which is very self-defeating, but rather as a normal — and forgivable — human imperfection. I learned this lesson from Rav Shlomo Greenstein, one of my father's close friends, a loyal *chassid* of the Bobover Rebbe, *shlita,* and a very learned man. He showed me that remembering things, even for a person who knows a great deal, is most often very hard work.

When I was studying in *Eretz Yisroel,* I once visited Rav Shlomo's family for *Shabbos.* There was a paragraph in the *Gur Aryeh* by the Maharal of Prague that I couldn't understand, so at the Shabbos table I asked some questions about it. Rav Shlomo surprised me by taking out the *sefer* and explaining the entire paragraph, word for word. I apologized for taking up so much of his time.

"Don't feel bad. When I teach something to someone else, I remember it forever," Rav Shlomo said.

"Forever is a long time," I replied. "How do you remember other things you learn?"

"Well, I used to remember the portion in the Gemara and its exact place on the page. Now that I'm getting older, I don't remember as well exactly where things are, so it takes me longer to look them up."

When he saw my look of wonder, Rav Shlomo said, "Memory isn't just something you are born with; it's something you work on. When I was in Yeshiva in Poland, *Shacharis* was at 7:00 and the Rebbe used to come in at 8:00. I had a study partner every morning. We would both wake up at 4:00 a.m. and spend *three hours reviewing* before the day started.

"After the war I worked full time running a lumber business in St. Paul, but I always learned at least three hours a day. Now I'm retired and have lots of time to learn. I attribute my ability to learn, *Boruch Hashem,* to the fact that I struggled to continue learning and to review, without interruption, all along."

It should be some comfort to know that even those who are born with better memories than others still need to review and to work at their learning in order to get things to stick in their minds.

Lastly, we should not overlook the fact that forgetting can be a blessing. I was reminded of this in one workshop by Baila who said, "Aren't there things you want to forget about?"

Sara Leah agreed. "When someone calls to apologize for insulting me and I can say I've forgotten about it, I feel great."

Miriam added, "I think that in order to go on with life optimistically you *must* forget what happened in the past."

I told her that the *Chovos Halevavos* agrees with her. In *Tehillim* 147:3, we read: הָרוֹפֵא לִשְׁבוּרֵי לֵב וּמְחַבֵּשׁ לְעַצְּבוֹתָם, *He heals the broken-hearted and mends their sorrows.* Rabbeinu Bachya says that הָרוֹפֵא means that it is actually Hashem Who heals. This refers to the fact that we are blessed with the natural healing of emotional wounds.

"If not for forgetting, one would never be relieved of sorrow. No joy could expel it from his mind, and nothing would afford him pleasure when he remembers the misfortunes of this world; he would hope for nothing and would not leave off brooding." (*Duties of The Heart,* The Gate of *Bechinah,* 5)

Rabbi Avigdor Miller explains: "[Forgetting] is a miraculous process of intricately planned wisdom, like a diary from which the unhappy episodes or words fade away, leaving only the pleasant entries. They do not merely fade, but the expressions change into words and phrases of a happier nature.

"Sometimes when misfortune comes, a man may feel it is impossible to go on, and he drops off to sleep in the blackest dejection. Yet in the morning he is a new man. What transpired during the night? A wondrous process, which we call "forgetting."

"Hashem has given you the power to forget and disregard the past. The past is gone forever and need never be brought to mind. Because you can forget, you are no longer disturbed by the past.

"The wonder of this process is rendered more remarkable when we note how it cooperates with the faculty of memory. The tragic knowledge of the previous day is not forgotten. All the details are faithfully registered in the mind. Yet the poignancy of the tragedy has paled overnight, the facts are more tolerable, and the attitudes of adjustment have begun to emerge. This process is one of the great kindnesses, and we are required to include it in our praise of Hashem, just as David did." (*Awake My Glory,* Rabbi Avigdor Miller)

"The two faculties of remembering and forgetting cause us to forget the unpleasant and to remember the pleasant, and thereby our lives are sweetened. We can consciously and voluntarily assist this process by concentrating our thoughts on remembering the kindness of Hashem to us, and by refusing to give time to remember our dissatisfactions. Only the useful should be remembered... An unkind word of a friend or husband or wife should **not** be remembered, but one **should not forget** their many kindnesses. Success in marriage and in all relationships requires a firm adherence to this precept. This is the proper attitude which makes society possible and enables men to continue to deal with each other" (*Rambam, De'os* 7:8).

We have a wonderful guarantee from Hashem that our memory will one day be restored to us. The *Zohar* (1:185a) tells us that in the future, Hashem will cause everyone to remember everything he ever learned, even if it was forgotten during his lifetime. In *Rabbi Nachman's Wisdom,* Rabbi Nachman of Breslov elaborates by saying that in the future life, all souls will remember and understand everything they heard and studied in this world, for Torah exists mainly for the soul. The happy person is one who fills his days with much Torah and devotion because it will eventually be restored to him.

We should learn from the promise in the *Zohar* the value of just doing as much as we can, even if time is limited and circumstances are difficult. Even if we can't understand everything we learn, even if we forget some of it, even if we have only a few minutes free, we should open a *sefer*. Think of it as making a deposit in a bank. The pennies add up, and the treasure we amass will be there for us. **We will one day remember everything.**

This has tremendous ramifications in the education of children and infants. Every word of Torah our children learn gives them a head start. Don't say, "They are only children, and they will forget it anyway." Talk Torah with your children, for one day it will return to them. The mother of the great sage, Rav Yehoshua Ben Chanania, who amazed not only his own people but also the gentiles of his era with his wisdom, brought his cradle into the house of learning so that as an infant, he would hear Torah. His teacher said: אַשְׁרֵי יוֹלַדְתּוֹ, "His mother should be praised." This is something we can do for our own children. We should also take heart ourselves, because if the baby will someday remember, then there is hope for us too!

In the meantime, in order not to get trapped in the frustration of forgetting, there are things we can do. Keep reading.

Exercise: Note-Taking Chart

Try to take notes in a way that fosters participation, growth and remembering instead of only writing. Here is a chart that you can xerox and use for just about any purpose: for a class, lecture, phone or cassette, even for a chapter that you have read in a book. Trying to focus on the main points in the material will help you remember it better.

Topic _____

Main Ideas:	Reactions:
1.————————	————————
————————	————————
2.————————	————————
————————	————————
3.————————	————————
————————	————————
4.————————	————————
————————	————————
5.————————	————————
————————	————————
6.————————	————————
————————	————————
7.————————	————————
————————	————————

Quotes to Remember:

1. ————————————————————

2. ————————————————————

Questions:

1. ————————————————————

2. ————————————————————

A Little Inner Joy Goes a Long Way

1. During a period when I was depressed, I became very absent-minded. Recently I heard Rabbi Pesach Krohn say that the letters of the word בְּשִׂמְחָה — *in happiness* — are the same as those in the word מַחֲשָׁבָה — *"thought."* I think that when we are cheerful, we remember things better.

2. It helps to pay attention in the first place. Try to feel curious about a person when you are introduced. I think the reason I forget people's names is not that I forgot them, but that I didn't hear them in the first place.

3. I write everything down.

4. Sometimes when you have forgotten something, it helps to relax and just accept it as part of Hashem's judgment. Once, on a freezing day as I walked out of the grocery, I realized that I didn't have the keys to the car. Only the week before my son had locked the keys inside, and we had to spend quite a bit of money to make new keys. I thought, "Perhaps Hashem is trying to tell me something." I remembered that when I was shopping, someone I knew had tried to talk to me, and I was unsympathetic; perhaps losing the keys was a gentle hint. I said, *"Gam zu l'tovah"* and promised to give money to the Rabbi Meir Baal HaNess *Tzedakah.* As I was about to leave the lot, I decided to have one more look in the store. I went to the candy aisle, and there they were, on top of the candy bin. It was an unbelievable thing; the keys appeared when I accepted Hashem's judgment with love. I was so elated.

5. Last summer a man from Russia came to visit his son in Camp Moodis, in Moodis, Connecticut. The son had been living in the States for about two years. He was learning in Yeshiva Ner Yisrael and hoped to introduce his father to religious life during his short stay. This father was a professor of philosophy. He would sit at the lectures in Moodis and mouth the speaker's words as he heard them, and afterward he could repeat every word. The rabbi who spoke on Shabbos met with him and wrote down the afternoon's lecture based on the professor's account.

6. The best way to remember a lesson or lecture is to teach it to someone else after you hear it.

7. Try to calm down if you are angry or upset. Once I had an appointment with the administrator of our school. I came in to find him in a panic. "My appointment book — I can't find my appointment book. This is terrible. Everyone's name is in it — the entire fall schedule is in it. I must have that book." I said, "Calm down. You probably know where it is but can't remember because you are upset." He looked on a shelf where he had looked before, and there it was, tucked between two other books.

8. Try to remain cheerful. You remember things better when you are in an upbeat mood.

9. Give some *tzedakah* to your favorite organization and ask Hashem to help you find a misplaced item.

10. Notice the things you *do* remember. I bet it happens at least twenty times a day!

Chapter 9
Rainy Days

It was a dull, gray, rainy morning when I went to see Chani in the hospital. I peeked into her room and saw her lying very quietly, staring pensively out of the window. As I entered her room, she turned her head. "Oh, Mrs. Shain! How very happy I am to see you."

I rushed over to her bedside and kissed her soundly on both cheeks. Casts fully covered both her legs. She was delighted with the book and the box of chocolates I had brought. I also gave her get-well cards from each of her classmates. She was anxious to hear all the news of school, and listened attentively to every word I said.

As I spoke to her, the pitter-patter of rain on her window seemed to beckon to us, and Chani ex-

claimed, *"How lovely the silvery raindrops are! You once said that special angels guide each raindrop from heaven to earth. How I wish to catch a raindrop with an angel still attached to it!"* (*Reaching for the Stars*, Ruchoma Shain).

The child in this story had an unusual insight. Rather than allowing the bad weather outside her window to dampen her mood she saw it as something spiritual. Instead of describing the raindrops as "gray," she described them as "silver."

What do you see when the raindrops fall? Do you see puddles, wet coats, and muddy roads? I also used to think of the rain as drab and depressing. But when I read this story I began to think that maybe there is more to it. Perhaps the rain is a symbol of blessing and wonder and abundance.

There are several reasons that we should smile on a rainy day. We can think about the great miracle of every individual raindrop, which is sent to us directly from Hashem. A rainy day is an auspicious time for prayers to be answered and requests to be granted. Finally, it is a day of opportunity. Hashem promises that on a rainy day especially, blessings for success in all your endeavors that day will shower upon you.

The preciousness of rain is backed up by the solid words of our Sages, who tell us that angels do indeed guide the raindrops: "May the name of the Creator be blessed and exalted, for He appoints one billion and ten thousand times ten thousand angels to tend to the rainfall. Every raindrop has its own special angel." (*Devarim Rabbah,* 7)

We learn further that there is no particle of the universe which is not invested with Divinity and special purpose. "Shlomo Hamelech said: *God founded the earth with wisdom; He established the heavens with circumspection* (*Mishlei* 3:19). This does not mean merely that the earth in general was fashioned with wisdom. This teaches that every component and every particle of the earth and the celestial bodies was created with the full measure of the Creator's wisdom. In order to fathom the secrets of the cell or of the atom, we would require a wisdom that is genius in scope. The planning and the purposefulness in our every cell and in our every atom is from the infinite wisdom of the Creator. Today we stand dumbfounded at what has been discovered about the complexity of the atom and the cell. Therefore, when the Rambam states (*Yesodei HaTorah* 2:2) that Hashem's wisdom in the physical world has no measure and no limit, he refers to the wisdom with which every atom and every cell has been invested." (*Sing, You Righteous*, Rabbi Avigdor Miller, p. 217).

The rain and wind patterns in the world not only reflect Hashem's wisdom, they demonstrate the incredibly interconnected design of the universe and remind us that we are part of a larger plan.

M.I.T. meteorologist, Edward Lorenz, wanted to know why the weather is so unpredictable. In 1963 he came up with a theory called the Butterfly Effect to explain this puzzle.

The theory states that increasing the number of weather stations and spreading them out to all the remote corners of the world would not enable us to predict the weather more than a month in advance. Even if we know all the precise details of the atmosphere at this moment, we cannot predict what conditions will be like in the future. Why? Because the most minute change in conditions at the beginning of an event multiplies enough to change the result dramatically. Lorenz used the example of a tiny butterfly flapping its wings in China, explaining that the effect of that slight breeze in China could multiply into a hurricane on the east coast three years later.

We can explain this same effect in spiritual terms. In the chapter *Borchi Nafshi* in *Tehillim* (104:4), David Hamelech says, עֹשֶׂה מַלְאָכָיו רוּחוֹת , *Hashem makes the winds His messengers*. The Butterfly Effect is an attempt of science to figure out a part of Hashem's complex plan. The breeze which we hardly notice acts upon many more segments of creation around the world.

When the rain interrupts our plans we are reminded that we are part of a larger plan, just like the wind and the rain.

Each raindrop is part of Hashem's plan for the entire universe. The rain that falls here may have originated on the other side of the globe, and it is impossible to know how it will affect the weather on the other side of the globe in a few months. Hashem coordinates each breeze and each moving cloud to provide rain and food for all the corners of the earth. What an awesome thought!

A rainy day is actually a day of blessing. Our Sages compare this to a king who sends gifts regularly to his son. Most of the time he sends the gifts with a messenger, but when he has something valuable to give, he invites his son to the palace, opens the treasury, and hands it over personally. Once the treasury doors are open, the child stands awed by all the beautiful gems and precious items inside, and if he is clever he will take the opportunity to request all he desires. And the father gladly gives. Why? The treasury is open, and he loves his child.

In the same way Hashem's benevolence is sent to us most of the time through angels, who follow His commands strictly. The rain, however, is so precious that it is not entrusted to a messenger. Hashem gives the rain personally from His treasury of good. When the treasury doors are open, He is close to us, and our Sages say that it is a favorable time for us to request whatever we want. We can ask to learn Torah as perceptively as our ancestors did at *Har Sinai,* and Hashem will grant us this wish. We can ask for redemption, for forgiveness, for health, for the return of the exiles — and Hashem will give to us from the treasury of good that is open when the rain falls. (*Book of Our Heritage, Cheshvan,* Eliyahu Kitov).

This is what it says in *Devarim* 28:12:   יִפְתַּח ה' לְךָ אֶת אוֹצָרוֹ הַטּוֹב, אֶת הַשָּׁמַיִם לָתֵת מְטַר אַרְצְךָ בְּעִתּוֹ וּלְבָרֵךְ אֵת כָּל מַעֲשֵׂה יָדֶךָ *Hashem will open His treasury of good in the Heavens, to give rain for your land at the right time, **and to bless all you do with your hands.***

Rabbi Avigdor Miller offers yet another hopeful perspective on rain, one that is obvious but often overlooked; he says that it is raining cherries and strawberries. If you think about that idea, you will see how true it really is. Everything needs water in order to grow — *even people*. We are composed of about 90% water.

I remember my parents talking about the rain when I was a little girl. Their thinking was very optimistic. We were once sitting around the tiny table in the kitchen, and my mother hurried to close the shutters because a storm had just erupted. She stood looking out at the lightning, thunder, and rain and said, "Thank God we have a roof over our heads. When we were running from city to city, only one step ahead of the Nazis, *yemach shemam*, there was no shelter from the rain. You just had to continue running."

My father glanced outside and said philosophically, "Rain in itself is also good. If it wouldn't rain, you wouldn't have what to eat." *Tehillim* speaks of this wonderful process: *He waters the mountains from the treasury in the Heavens; from the fruit of Your works the earth's thirst is quenched* (*Tehillim* 104:13). The most vital blessing that comes down with the rain is food. The wheat that eventually becomes flour and bread, the grass eaten by the cows, who in turn provide us with milk and meat (not together, of course), and the 260 different types of fruits and vegetables available in the average supermarket all grew because it rained.

We take the rain and our food for granted and remain discontented, because our minds are busy with our other problems, but each meal could be elevated into a ceremony of service to Hashem if we took the time to properly appreciate the food and its source. The Sages instructed us to make a blessing over rain three times a day and over each food so that we should appreciate this important relationship.

There is an interesting painting on the wall in my parents' dining room. It shows a bare wood table on which lie half a loaf of old, dry bread, a knife, a large slice of watermelon, two young onions, and a clay jug. It's not a very pretty picture, although it was well done and the food looks real. I always wondered about it, and one day I asked my father, "Why is this painting in the dining room?"

"When I lived in Samarkand in Russia during World War

II," he replied, "every day of life was a gift. There were many times when I was hungry and I wasn't sure if I would pull through. That painting represents a big meal in Samarkand. If you had that much food to eat at one time, you felt like making a party.

"When I sit at the *Shabbos* table each week, and I'm surrounded by your mother and your sister and brother, and your mother brings out one delicious dish after another, and we are comfortable, and we have peace, and the silver candlesticks and the silver Kiddush cup on the white tablecloth smile to me — I try not to take one bite for granted. Each week I thank Hashem that He rescued me from there and brought me here."

Each time my father says a *berachah* in a loud, clear voice and glances at the painting, he is nourished by the attitude that rain, food, peace, health, family, and all the other blessings he enjoys are a gift from Hashem.

Practice this attitude before you say a *berachah*. Are you holding a delicious orange or golden peach in your hand? Think about the wind and the rain that nourished the peach tree and helped it grow. Think about all the forces that Hashem coordinated to bring that peach to you. You will learn not only a different response to rain, but you will be in a better mood all the time.

When one supplements his meals with gratitude, the results are remarkable. Remember that each raindrop brings a present for you from Hashem. Review the evidence of the benefits of rain, and you can enhance the quality of your life. As the Rebbe of Kobrin *zt"l* says, "You are where your thoughts are."

Finally, we can turn our attention to the practical aspects of a rainy day. What should we do with ourselves when it's pouring outside?

Most people feel saddened by stormy weather because it limits their activity. They see rain as an obstacle for which they can never be fully prepared. However, although it is difficult "to swim" through the rain, it isn't impossible. Everyone else may be staying in bed, but you can have a constructive day. You can spend time with friends indoors or do an interesting project on your own. Even clearing out rubble on the bottom of your closet or taking care of the bills that were piling up will make you feel productive.

With a little determination you can mobilize your resources and get outdoors too. When there is something important to accomplish, one needn't be stopped by the weather. Rochel's story describes the power of inner enthusiasm in overcoming the elements:

"There was a terrible snowstorm. Part of the time it was raining, part of the time it was hailing, and part of the time it was windy and snowing. I went to visit a good friend of mine from across the street who was now very sick in the hospital. She had cancer, but I didn't know it then. During the visit, I had a feeling that she needed something extra to lift her spirits. I told her I would make her blintzes.

"When I finally got home from the hospital, after plowing through the storm, I was exhausted. I checked the refrigerator, and I was shocked! I didn't have any of the ingredients for the blintzes. No flour, no sugar, no eggs, no farmer cheese. I usually have these things in the house, but today, I didn't. I looked out. There was no sign of the storm letting up. In such weather you don't even go out to a neighbor, that's how bad it was. I wondered if I could borrow the ingredients, but people don't usually have farmer cheese on hand on an ordinary weekday. And anyway, if I was going out for that, I might as well shop for all the ingredients.

"The store is on the corner, but the snow was knee high and the wind was blowing in my face. But you know what? I went so quickly! In five minutes I was at the corner, and in five minutes I was back. I think I had springs in my feet. I really wanted to do this *mitzvah*, and nothing was going to stop me. I made the blintzes and carried them across the street to her husband. He was so surprised! 'In this weather you did it?!' he said to me.

"My friend really loved the blintzes, and the gift restored some of her usual good cheer. I keep thinking about that awful storm. I was so enthusiastic about my project that I really didn't notice it. Everything is in a person's head."

We can also get up and get going despite the rain. Have you ever found that once you decided to accomplish a specific deed the weather didn't stop you? You thought that a successful day was ruined, but find the opposite. The constructive action you take when things seem bleak on the surface can improve your health and make you a more sensitive parent or a more caring friend.

How can you enjoy yourself while you face the rain?

Exercise: A Constructive Rainy Day

Now for some of your own ideas. What can you do to have a cheerful constructive rainy day? Plan ahead now, so that you can wake up on a gray morning with a pleasant goal.

_____

_____

_____

_____

_____

_____

_____

_____

_____

_____

_____

A Little Inner Joy Goes a Long Way

Practical Tips for a Rainy Day

Here are some steps you can take offered by women in the workshop to have an energetic, optimistic and productive rainy day.

Surie:

1. Get dressed in bright, happy colors like sunshine yellow, and smile when you look in the mirror.
2. Go out in the rain. Smell the special freshness in the air and see the crystal raindrops. Feel the essence of nature.
3. "Splash" in the puddles and allow yourself to feel some childish curiosity again.

Mimi:

1. Write a letter.
2. Call someone you haven't called for a while.
3. Read a Torah book.

Nechama:

1. Go out for a walk in the rain without an umbrella and think of the raindrops on your face as a caress from Hashem.
2. I call my mother and talk to her — and *listen to her.*
3. Cook or bake something so the house smells good, and make a soup for your husband so he will feel good after working all day.

Judy:

1. I keep a scrap book with inspirational sayings. Whenever I see something nice, like a pretty picture or an inspiring article, I cut it out and keep it in a special drawer. A rainy day is a good time to take these scraps out, cut them up, and arrange them in the book.

Leah:

1. Be prepared to go out. Be sure you have an umbrella, coat and boots. Don't stay indoors if it makes you feel locked in.
2. Don't stay in bed. Make sure to find some constructive things to do, even if you are forced to change your plans. After all, the final decision on the kind of day you will have *has to be yours.*

Chapter 10
Morning

"**M**e, feel confident and productive in the morning? That's a good joke."

"At one a.m. I become joyous. In the morning I am blah."

"By the time the last child is safely out the door, I'm about ready to collapse."

"I promise myself a short nap in the afternoon to motivate me to get out of bed early."

"I laugh when I think of it: my neighbor in the bungalow colony would dress her children in their clothes for the next morning instead of in pajamas!"

"Don't call me before twelve. I'm so groggy early in the day that people who speak to me think I've got the flu. I always wonder how I will get through the day."

The women in the workshop were very open, as you can

see, about their morning feelings. I hope it comforts you to realize from these remarks that it is normal to have a battle with your urge to sleep when the alarm clock rings in the morning. We all share the same problem. Morning is the hardest period of the day for many of us. Rav Eliyahu Lopian explains that waking up is a struggle because the morning hours are such a crucial time and the *yetzer hara* is always out to sabotage times of potential holiness.

Our mood in the morning has a ripple effect. The beginning determines what the rest of the day will be like. During your regular activities — pushing your stroller, walking in and out of stores, picking up your child at the bus stop — you will continually reproduce your morning mood. Creating a pleasant, productive morning routine takes effort, but it's worth it.

The first step is to get out of bed, preferably early — even if it hurts! If you let go and turn over, half an hour will slip away before you realize you've overslept. If you grab yourself at the first instant, you won't be sorry. It is a very wise investment, and you will feel the returns throughout the day. When Rabbi Simchah Zissel of Kelm would wake up his young children in the morning, he would gently say to them, "Children, here you are sleeping when you have a kingdom to rule. The Almighty gave man rulership over the entire creation" (*Meoros Hagedolim*).

There are three vital tactics that you can use to help you get a good start in the morning. The very first thing to do is to wake up with joy. Some people begin their day with an energy boost by drinking a vitamin mix. You can achieve exactly the same result by filling yourself with grateful and joyous thoughts. Fill up your lungs with a delicious scent by holding on to the simple moments you've enjoyed. Savor those common little things you have almost forgotten. You will feel simultaneously that you are exhaling uneasiness and after a few minutes of ruminating you will see a garden of roses where before there was only cement. You will feel that just as Hashem has granted you this new day, He will bolster you always. As King David said when he was running for his life from Avshalom:

אֲנִי שָׁכַבְתִּי וָאִישָׁנָה הֱקִיצוֹתִי כִּי ה' יִסְמְכֵנִי , *I lay down and slept, yet I awoke, for Hashem supports me* (*Tehillim* 3:6).

You will feel ready to receive the blessing Hashem has prepared for you today if you think about this verse and its significance. There is an exercise at the end of the chapter that can help prepare you to greet the new day with joy.

Part of being joyful is to pat yourself on the back. This is also a wonderful thing to do as the day begins, and it will give you a hopeful outlook. As Miriam commented, "If you are down on yourself in the morning, you will never get out of the hole. Once a self-critical thought gets wedged in your mind, your energy dissipates like the bubbles that float out of seltzer. You should ask yourself, 'What do I do right?' Instead of groaning that you never know where the children's socks are, congratulate yourself because you always give them a kiss, sing *Modeh Ani* out loud with them, and send them off with a cheerful farewell and a blessing that Hashem should help them. Don't say, 'I'm not good at that.' Think instead of the many things you do well. A person goes מֵחַיִל אֶל חָיִל, *from strength to strength.*

The second strategy for starting a good day is especially important: pray. The soul needs to be revived just as the body does. Here is Rav Yonasan Eibeshitz's prescription for a healthy day that is quoted by Rav Eliyahu Lopian:

> *Behold, the first hours of the day are crucial. If a person manages to sanctify the beginning, the entire day will become holy. With what should one start his day? Pray sincerely. Our sages warn that prayer needs strengthening, because the yetzer labors to trip the person up and to plunder the decisiveness of the morning.*
>
> *Who is greater than Rav Yonasan Eibeshitz zt"l? He authored more than thirty sefarim brimming with true wisdom, besides his famous sefarim in Jewish Law. In his sefer Ya'aros Devash he testifies: "On a day when I prayed very well in the morning, the*

entire day's learning and teaching went well." One must be strong and rise to pray in the morning with enthusiasm. Put in every effort to make the beginning of the day especially good and especially holy. May Hashem help us to honor His Name. (Lev Eliyahu, Bereishis)

The prayers that we say in the morning support the effectiveness of joyful thoughts. In *Ashrei* it is written: זֵכֶר רַב טוּבְךָ יַבִּיעוּ, וְצִדְקָתְךָ יְרַנֵּנוּ, *The remembrance of Your great goodness they* [every Jew] *shall utter, and of Your righteousness they will sing exultantly.* The word ,יַבִּיעוּ, *they will utter,* also means to overflow and pour out. Reminding ourselves of Hashem's many kindnesses to us is therapeutic, for it causes an overflow of good feeling. Rabbi Avigdor Miller tells us that a person should constantly remember and repeat the benefits that Hashem bestows on all mankind and on him individually. He should thank Hashem for all that he and his forebears received: "The accumulation of the memory of the many kindnesses of Hashem fills his heart to the brim. If a person consciously remembers Hashem's kindness, any additional happiness or good fortune causes an overflow of joy and gratitude. However, if one has a "hole in his cup" because he fails to remember all the great and little successes and joys which he experienced, then his cup can never be full and can never run over with happiness and gratitude. Their happiness evaporates by forgetfulness and their cup is always empty. (*Praise My Soul,* Rabbi Avigdor Miller, p. 128)

Prayer should be very personal. I try to make a list before I start the prayers, reminding myself to pay attention to the specific things Hashem helped me with yesterday and asking for His assistance with today's plans. Think of the pleasant experience that you brought to mind as you woke up and thank Him for that too.

Tell Hashem in your prayers that you will try just a little bit harder today. Rebbetzin Esther Greenberg said, "Wake up in the morning and formally invite Hashem's Presence into your home. Where there is peace, the *Shechinah* (Hashem's Presence) dwells. Tell yourself that today you won't raise your voice or criticize the children publicly or speak gossip. Today you will be patient, and Hashem will be with you."

"When a person accepts upon himself the service of Hashem in the morning, this resolution will cause all his actions of the day to be aligned with the true good." (*Sfas Emes, Bechukosai*)

At this point, when you are in a calm and hopeful mood, it is time to focus on the day ahead. Looking ahead for even a moment or two and using positive visualization can help us immeasurably. Think about what you have to do today and try to picture yourself handling it smoothly and cheerfully. Your prophecy is bound to be self-fulfilling.

Rabbi Avigdor Miller advises us:

> *Choose a minute and think, "What is going to happen in the next ten minutes of my life?" It's a big job. You can't know what is going to happen. Think, however, of the possibilities and plan the best reaction to all eventualities. Try to do this once a day for one minute.*
>
> *You are on the way to a wedding. Your son or daughter is getting married that night. You have already met the parents of the bride or groom, and now you will meet the entire family. Think how you will react as you meet each person. At a wedding everyone is excited. There is never a wedding without someone being offended. You have to be prepared. It's a gift to have even a few minutes of foresight.*
>
> *When a Secretary of State has to formulate a statement, he calls all the diplomats and advisers at the Pentagon and consults with them before he makes that statement.*
>
> *The Tannaim looked ahead before each deed and thought of its ramifications all their days and*

in the World to Come. It's good to start off by giving yourself a minute to look ahead. (Tape No. 730, Rabbi Avigdor Miller)

I remember one particular morning before we left on a trip to visit my parents. I knew from experience that car trips can be a hassle, and I decided to put myself in a positive mood by mentally running through the day. When I woke up I decided that I would modulate my voice and keep it low; that I would not expect to be exactly on time, that I would be encouraging to the children and to my husband and give them space; that I would remember to give *tzedakah* and kiss the *mezuzah* before I went out to the car.

In fact, I follow this routine on the morning before every lecture. There is always an abundance of possible worries before a workshop, but I try instead to envision a peaceful session: There will be at least ten people there; I'll remember to return the books people left on the table last week; there will be a lively discussion; I'll keep a sick person in mind and dedicate the lecture to him; I'll show my approval when I answer questions and make everyone feel good; I will be patient and not arrogant when the audience stops my lecture with particularly loud conversation.

I have found that calm visualization really helps prepare me to meet the day's challenges, and it can work for you too. Even if you have been up all night with an infant, or you have been lying awake with worries on your mind, you can still wake up with a hopeful heart. At the start of the day, think about each event that will occur and form a mental image of your best option. See yourself remaining composed in the doctor's office, passing your driver's test, or having a calm discussion with the boiler repairman. Imagine yourself doing everything right the first time. See yourself with a smile on your face and a relaxed, happy disposition.

Those first moments when we emerge from slumber are a wonderful opportunity for renewal. We receive this gift each and every morning, and we can give ourselves an additional bonus by deciding optimistically, "Just for today, I will start to be all I've dreamed of being."

Have you perhaps been muttering to yourself, "This is fine for people who have a natural rhythm of early rising, but I'm just not that type?" If mornings are difficult for you, you will have to plan in advance for a positive experience. By investing effort the day before to focus on times you woke up with energy in the past and to prepare a pleasant atmosphere for tomorrow, you will lay the foundation for a morning of joy and ease.

Completing one successful morning provides proof that we are capable of doing so. Even after a lifetime of unsatisfactory mornings, success can reverse our unfavorable memories. With each additional successful rising we feel less sluggish, and soon we begin to think grateful thoughts spontaneously from the first moment that we are awake.

Exercise:
Part I: A Good Morning Memory

Can you remember a specific morning when you had no trouble getting up — a time when you were energetic and enthusiastic, and as a result your day went well? Write a description of that morning and of everything that was going on in your head.

_____

_____

_____

True Responses: "Good Morning!"

1. I woke up early last Friday to cook and bake for Shabbos. I asked Hashem for the *challos* and all the other food to come out good. A close friend who was staying with us for Shabbos called to say she had just arrived from Montreal. "Did I wake

you?" she asked. It felt good to say that I'd been up for a while already.

2. I decided to work on my *davening* during the month before Rosh Hashanah. I woke up at six each day to be able to speak to Hashem in complete peace and quiet. It left a sweet taste in my mind for the rest of the day. Perhaps I will continue to do it at least a few times a week all year.

3. Last year my husband bought me a *sefer* that I really wanted to learn. My first thought was, "Oh, it's too big — I'll never get through it." It wasn't the type of book that you just read; you had to concentrate to truly gain anything. I decided to read just three pages a day while I drank my morning coffee. It gave me something pleasant to think about all day. By the end of the year I did finish the *sefer*.

4. I wonder where the energy came from when I was a *kallah*. I woke up early every morning the week before the wedding because I wanted to finish the entire *Sefer Tehillim*. On the morning of the wedding I didn't shout at anyone, despite many minor things that went wrong. For example, I noticed there was a spot on my wedding gown, but I took it in stride. I was just so happy that it didn't matter to me. It was a great week.

5. When I started the Shalheves learning center in Monsey, I woke up early to hang posters. I had to hang up the posters because no one else wanted to do it. I feel more comfortable doing this when there aren't ten people milling around watching me, so I got up early and arrived in the neighborhood at about eight o'clock when things were still quiet. I had brought along some cheap masking tape and it didn't work well. There I was standing on a street corner hanging up signs, and the tape kept on splitting. I couldn't even run into a store to buy more tape because nothing was open except the grocery store. So I said, "Hashem, I want to try — help me. At least the tape shouldn't tear." For the rest of the morning the tape worked fine. But you want to know something else? That entire day went well in an extra special way.

6. I got up very early in the morning and baked six cakes and

200 *rugelach* for my son's *aufruf*. I said to myself, "Look, it has to be done. Either lie in bed, or get up and do it." So I got up and prayed, "*Ribono Shel Olam*, help me." And He did.

7. I am a high-school teacher. Once they asked me on Thursday night to speak on Monday morning at an assembly for the entire school. I had to be there at ten. I woke up early and *davened Shacharis*. You know the saying about being so busy you just better have time to pray. Then I ran to get my *sheitel* done. The hairdresser gave me an appointment on ten minutes' notice. Then I went to pick up a new maternity dress for the event that was coming later that day. The lady who sells them in her house had agreed to let me pick it up early. After that, I dropped off my children at the home of a good friend who had agreed to babysit that morning. I still got to the assembly ten minutes early!

Part II: A Joyful Wake-Up

"How do I create that first glowing morning?" you might wonder.

Every person has problems. We often wake up thinking of the things that bother us and this generates even more negative expectations for the day ahead. However, if one makes a conscious effort he can usually find some good things that have happened recently as well; and if they happened last week despite one's problems, nice things can happen again today. The morning is the most potent time for planting these seeds of optimism.

Rabbi Abraham Twerski has written a series of Torah books based on the calendar that many people keep at their bedsides. They have found that an inspiring thought helps them start their day in the right way. You can take this a step further by keeping a small memo pad near your bed in which you record your personal successes and affirmations. Another option is to put a letter, photograph, or other meaningful item near your bed where you can see it when you first open your eyes. It will help a great deal if you decide the night before what you are going to think about when you wake up. In the morning, grogginess and fatigue tend to dominate our minds and it is harder to generate pleasant thoughts. But if the thought is prepared in advance, we can latch onto it the moment we open our eyes.

Here is a chart to jog your memory about pleasant experiences. Of course it is only a partial listing.

Think Back to a Time When You:

Did something very different, or differently	Were helped by someone	Accomplished something difficult
Received good news	Had a good time with a child	Received a pleasant surprise
Made someone else happy	Gained insight	Overcame a negative trait
Dealt well with conflict	Received a gift	Received or sent a letter
Met someone you admired	Had a sunny day outdoors	Had a good conversation

1. With your eyes closed, state out loud the scene you chose to think about. For example, if you chose gaining insight, you would say aloud, "I'm going to think about the lecture I was at last week."

(This may sound a bit childish at first, but the truth is that many of us habitually talk to ourselves when no one else is around. If we are doing it anyway, why not give ourselves helpful ideas?)

2. Imagine at least five details of your scene. In our example, you

might picture the room, your seat, the size of the audience, what the atmosphere was like, and the appearance of the speaker.

3. Before you open your eyes, take your emotional temperature. Do you feel more relaxed?

4. Now write four sentences describing the experience. Leave these jottings near your bed so that you can read them when you wake up tomorrow morning.

_____

_____

_____

_____

True Responses: A Joyful Wake-Up

1. **Good Time With a Child:** Yesterday my Breindy got sneakers. Now she walks with tights and shoes. I have a supply of clothes for her from gifts and family hand-me-downs. My sister has six girls, and she gave me a knit dress that was in style fifteen years ago. I decided to put it on her today. She's my first girl after seven sons, and I wanted to see how she looked in it. She looked like a living doll! I was so excited and so happy. I called my sister. She said, "That dress! Everyone will know it's a hand-me-down. It's so dated." I replied, "You don't understand. I've wanted to see a daughter in this dress for fifteen years." I'm going to pick another dress for her to wear tomorrow and put it near my bed. I know I'll smile when I see it.

2. **Gift:** Someone gave me a lovely photo frame for helping out with her child. I walk her child home from the bus every day. It felt good to see that people appreciate the little things you do for them. I was wondering where I'd put it . Now I'll put it where I can see it when I wake up.

3. **Accomplishment:** I learned how to sew, and I have finished a few articles of clothing for my children. It feels good to have a new talent, and knowing that I will have some time tomorrow to sew gives me a treat to anticipate.

4. **Accomplishment:** I made nicer suppers this week. That takes planning because I work full time. When I feel down about leaving my crying toddler I can remind myself of the pleasant evening we will have.

5. **Letter:** My son just became Bar Mitzvah. Of course we sent invitations to our cousins overseas. They just sent back a letter wishing us *mazel tov* and included some pictures from years ago in the envelope. I'm planning to slide them into my mirror frame. It will be a nice thing to wake up to tomorrow.

6. **Letter:** My daughter who lives in Yerushalayim with her husband and four children sent me a fax. It showed an ad in the Jerusalem Post for AMIT "Lunch and Learn." My daughter is the chairlady of this lecture series. I usually put these letters in a desk drawer and forget about them, but it is a good idea to keep it on my night table for several days.

7. **Pleasant News:** A friend of mine who has been a widow for eleven years remarried. The thought behind this good news is that Hashem watches over and helps everyone. Even if they were in trouble at times, they will have some happiness too. It is a very encouraging thought to wake up to.

8. **Overcoming a Negative Trait:** I went to visit my daughter-in-law and her house was a mess. Instead of criticizing I did all her dishes. I'm going to remember tomorrow morning that our relationship is improving.

9. **Pleasant Surprise:** Yesterday I sent my son to take out his *Rashi* sheet from his backpack. He had left his sheet in school but he had received a certificate for being the "Best Student of The Month" which he showed me. It was a lovely surprise. Then he got some scotch tape and hung it up in my room.

10. **Sunny Day Outdoors:** My friend, who has a huge van, took me and my three youngest children to a really nice park last week. It was a treat for all of us, because the children aren't in day camp. The little ones played in the sandbox and ran in the grass. My friend and I sat on the park bench and watched them happily enjoying their freedom. They brought

home leaves and stones that they made into a picture for me. I hung the picture above my bed.

11. **New Experience:** I went away with a friend to a weekend Torah conference that was sponsored by Chabad Women of America. It was in the Midwest, in a city I'd never been to before. The conference was not elaborate, but everything was thoughtfully organized from beginning to end, and the lectures were stimulating and practical. I took notes and highlighted the main points with a pink highlighter. I need only glance at a sentence or two in the mornings to remember the delicious experience.

12. **Dealing Well With Conflict:** I just did the hardest thing in the world — I called someone and apologized for embarrassing her in public. I was in a store, and as I waited on line I made a casual comment that was somewhat derogatory, and I saw that the owner changed color. So I called her and apologized last night.

13. **Good Conversation:** I've been married for twelve years, but I only got to know my husband's aunt for the first time last week. We had invited her and her husband to be our guests at my son's yeshiva dinner. My aunt sat next to me and told me how her family had escaped Germany shortly before World War II. She described the many miracles God had performed for them during their escape. I later found out that she hadn't told this story to any other relatives. I feel honored that she told it to me.

14. **Meeting Someone Admirable:** I knew a woman named Seffi, *a"h*, who had a kidney condition. Seffi had had two transplants which failed and lived most of her life with no kidneys; she endured dialysis three times a week. She had lost her father when she was a young girl, when her mother was expecting her younger brother.

One could not find a more sensitive, caring, and intelligent person than Seffi. She loved learning, went to lectures, and asked questions. She loved Hashem's world; she painted and drew and photographed everything around her with great thought and emotion. She joined in everyone's celebrations. She didn't go around brooding. She had such a positive outlook and set an example for all those who knew her. She didn't feel sorry for herself, but was grateful for every small, good thing that happened.

15. **Receiving Help:** I was a new teacher, and I was extremely nervous. Teaching was something I really wanted to do, and I knew I had potential, but I had very little idea how to handle a classroom. The assistant principal and I lived in the same neighborhood, and she offered to take me home after school. Every evening for nearly a year I got into that car with a list of questions, and she gave me private teacher training. She was never impatient and offered me constant encouragement. It is thanks to her that I became a successful teacher. When I wake up in the morning, I think about how much I am looking forward to the day in school.

16. **Made Someone Else Happy:** A good friend of mine got her driver's license recently. She had waited for this for a long time, and it was a big milestone for her. I baked her a special cake and invited several friends over on Shabbos afternoon for the "unveiling." The cake was in the shape of a car, and it was fully equipped: it had toothpick windshield wipers, tinfoil windows, mint candy headlights, and a license plate with my friend's name on it. I had even improvised a parking meter with some "grass" growing in front of it. It was by no means a professional job, but it *was* cute. My friend had a good laugh, and she was thrilled to have someone share in her achievement.

17. **Gained Insight:** I began going to a small *Navi shiur* recently. The man who teaches it is excellent, and he presents the subject much differently than I ever learned it before. When we learned *Navi* in high school or seminary, the people portrayed in the text seemed very saintly and beyond reach. He presents them as real human beings who had many of the same feelings and conflicts that we do. Without diminishing

their greatness, he makes them accessible. I feel much closer to the *Navi* than I did when I was younger, and better able to absorb lessons from it.

A Little Inner Joy Goes a Long Way

Practical Tips for the Morning

1. Remember that you are a servant of Hashem. The *Shulchan Aruch* tells us that when a person gets up in the morning, he is like a newly created being. This is why we wash our hands, in imitation of the *Kohanim*, who used to wash their hands from a special basin in order to sanctify themselves before their service in the *Beis Hamikdash*. It is good when we wake up to think of ourselves as people who have been chosen for a special mission.

2. Eat breakfast. Our Sages tell us that one who waits to eat breakfast until the noon hour may feel full, but he will not get all the nutritional benefits of the food.

3. Get dressed neatly. Put on earrings and an attractive kerchief. It will help your family, and it will make you feel good.

4. Perhaps you are trying to squeeze too much into the morning. Prepare your clothes the night before, or take care of some other small task that will make the following morning smoother.

5. Don't shout! Rav Elya Lopian, *zt"l* said, "When you wake a person up with shouting and threats, you ruin his day."

Chapter 11
Rush Hour

Chana was rushing around the house, finishing two or three last-minute chores before the children came home. The music was on, and at first she didn't hear the doorbell ring. By the time she realized, she could hear her son kicking at the door full force. She opened the door and he flew in, threw down his briefcase and screamed, "Why didn't you come to the door? It's snowing outside."

Chana thought to herself, "What makes him get so angry? I've had a good day and I don't want to struggle with this. Why should his mood drag me down now?" Before she knew what had happened Chana began screaming at her son for his lack of respect. The evening went downhill after that.

Scenes like this are fairly common in the average family. The time as you might have guessed is "rush hour," the hour right before dinner. It is a peak stress time in many homes, the point where all the day's tensions accumulate. Parents are tired after a day of work at home or at the office. The house is in limbo; a look at the half-prepared supper, the cluttered table, the pile of laundry, and the scattered briefcases makes us feel overwhelmed and irritable. Our children have been separated from us all day, and now they want extra attention. They want to tell us about their worries, problems, and joys, but they can't catch us. Because they are hungry and low on energy, they begin to quarrel with each other. Somehow we feel that there is only one person to take care of everything right now: Us! Where do we begin?

Does this pressure often cause a volcanic eruption in your home?

"I can tell right away when my husband has had a difficult day," Sara said. "His shoulders are hunched, I can barely hear him say hello, his eyes look sad, and he kicks a child's toy out of the way with extra force. If I ask him what happened, he'll say he doesn't want to upset me by talking about it. When I see him so dejected, I feel grouchy too."

Sara's last comment pinpoints an important emotional phenomenon and one that kicks in heavily during rush hour: everywhere and at all times, feelings are contagious. Whether at a party, in the classroom, at the office, or at the dinner table, emotions drift from one person to another. As King Solomon said in *Mishlei* (27:19): כַּמַּיִם הַפָּנִים לַפָּנִים, כֵּן לֵב הָאָדָם לָאָדָם, *As the water reflects the face you present to it, so the feelings of the heart reflect from one person to the other.*

Metzudas David explains, "The water will show you a reflection of the face looking into it. If it sees a smiling face, it smiles back. If it sees a sad face, the water looks sad. So it is with people's hearts. If a person is cheerful, the person next to him will try to feel good, and if a person shows sadness, the other person will feel bad as well."

Rabbi Chaim Zaitchik tells us in *Sparks of Mussar* that Aharon HaCohen was a successful peacemaker because he was able to employ this principle: "Aharon, Moshe's brother, was a master at making peace between people. He had intense love for each person, and with this great love he was able to motivate other people to have love for each other. Flames of love came from his heart and entered the hearts of everyone else. Use this as your model when you work on making peace."

This instinctive imitation has a physiological basis. Paul Elkman Ph.D., professor of psychology at the University of California Medical School in San Francisco, asserts, "A neurological reaction allows you to pick up others' emotions. When you are around angry people, for example, you unconsciously signal your brain's cortex (which controls facial movements) to mimic their lowered eyebrows, tensed lips, and glaring eyes. That signal is transmitted to your hypothalamus, [the portion of the brain] which controls emotions, and triggers the same reaction in you."

In short, we tune into other people's feelings and unconsciously mimic them. This is the reason we all try to seek out friends who will lift our spirits. We are lucky if we can call on someone whose cheerful greetings and funny story will make us laugh. Even when we see children laughing and playing, it can make us grin. However, it's not enough to remain in neutral and wait for someone else to lift us up. We've got to make a conscious effort to start the positive cycle by taking the initiative and being the first to offer a loving heart and a smile.

At no time is this more important than during rush hour, when all the members of the family converge upon us, ready to unload the brunt of the day's activities. They will be looking to us to gauge the emotional temperature in the household, as well as to provide comfort and encouragement.

At first this may seem like a heavy load to bear, especially if we have had a difficult day ourselves. Our first thought may be: "Why me?"

Yaffa Ganz explains eloquently that women have a special gift for nurturing others: "Women are more than just strong. They are smart and loving, sympathetic and joyful and creative. They are endowed with certain instinctive gifts whose

exact definition has eluded scientific analysis to this day —
the *binah yeseirah* (extra understanding) which our Sages
mentioned a few thousand years ago, and the special
neshamah which God crafted for them to function as the *ezer*,
that indispensable partner to man.

"As part of their unique equipment, women have special
antennae which run like long threads throughout human history and society, keeping them finely attuned to the needs of
the people they know and love. The information they supply
helps make our world a happier, better, and more heavenly
place." (*All Things Considered,* Yaffa Ganz p. 15)

Of course it's no secret to us that women are good at nurturing. But it's especially important for us to remember our
unique ability to calm others down and make them feel good
at a time during the day when we would like a little nurturing
ourselves.

Ironically, the initial effort we make sends out ripples that
return to us. I'm reminded of a story that Rina told me: "I had
promised my students from the Russian adult class that I'd
sing and play guitar for them at our Chanukah party. That day
I had a personal setback and was feeling sad. However, I
pushed myself to sing and taught them four Chanukah songs.
They did so well that I took them to another class to show
them off. The other teacher played the piano, and everyone
sang and danced. A third class joined us, and the singing and
dancing continued for three hours. I really felt good and actually walked out smiling."

Notice that Rina not only cheered up the Russian adults,
but she herself walked out smiling. In the *Mesilas Yesharim,*
Rabbi Moshe Chaim Luzatto asserts: "A good recommenda-
tion for one who wants to awaken his natural enthusiasm is
that enthusiasm comes from doing. One's outward expressions and actions awaken his inner feelings. A person defi-
nitely has more control over his outer self than his inner self.
Through willing himself to quicken his outer movements, there
will arise within him an inner joy."

Does this mean that if you smile when your family comes

home at the end of the day, they'll all wind up dancing in the aisle? Perhaps not. But the principle holds true. The people around you are likely to reflect back what they see in you. There is something about a smile that softens people. And even if you are not feeling very smiley yourself by the time rush hour rolls around, the sense of calm that you exude, even if you have to fake it, will benefit you as well.

Younger children especially need your attention when they come home. Although it may be difficult for you to focus on their feelings and demands, you may feel less resistant when you consider what they have been through during the day.

Think about it. After a hurried breakfast of cereal and milk, your child boards a noisy, crowded bus for the sometimes long ride to school. The teacher has a different subject or activity scheduled every half hour. The day is full of instructions that must be obeyed immediately: "Take out your books, pass down the sheet, get ready for lunch, line up in a straight line double-file against the wall." Challenges abound: "Can you find your homework pad? Can you keep your finger on the place in the book throughout the lesson? Can you answer a difficult question? Can you catch all the spelling words as they are dictated? Did you make sure to have your test paper signed?" With thirty-two children in the class, there isn't much time to listen to individual questions or talk with any one child.

Have you stopped to think about the type of feedback your child is receiving during this hectic, fast-paced day? In 1982 a researcher was assigned a group of one hundred children and asked to record how many negative and positive comments each received during the course of the day. Her findings were that on average, each child received 460 negative or critical comments and only 75 positive or supportive comments! (*Quantum Learning*, p. 24). Your day at home probably hasn't been quite as stressful.

After a long session at school, your child comes home and rings the bell. Shouldn't he get a free smile and a good word from you?

It is vital at this time for the family to take a fifteen minute-break together before continuing with any activities on your list. Fifteen minutes seems like a long time at the end of the day but it is well-spent time. You will have a chance to reconnect to your children and find out what happened in school, and they will get the attention they need to keep them going until dinner.

Some parents serve an appetizer — a portion of a side dish that they prepared for supper. Others serve healthful snacks that won't ruin anyone's appetite such as a salad or some fruit. This will help everyone wait a little more patiently until supper is ready. We can quietly talk and take a rest from the pressures of the day. Some music that the family enjoys can add to the peace of the atmosphere. Once we've taken time for this short break the children can try an independent activity and we can put all the pieces of the house and supper together. This can help everyone enjoy their responsibilities instead of struggling through them.

When we talked about mornings, we discussed the benefits of planning ahead to have a pleasant awakening, since it is too difficult to structure ourselves when our bodies are telling us something different. Planning ahead is also invaluable during rush hour.

Our main goal is to give this time of day one hundred percent of ourselves. We all want to speak calmly, wait before acting when the children misbehave, and repeat instructions without getting nervous. We know that our good mood is nourishment for the tired souls around us, yet we must also keep in mind that we are only human. There will still be times when things seem to fall apart, but we will notice that there are many more good days than bad ones, and that our children are calmer and happier.

Following are some suggestions from workshop participants that have proven effective in managing the potential chaos of the coming-home hour.

A Little Inner Joy Goes a Long Way

===== **Practical Tips** =====

1. Try to have everyone do their homework as soon as they come home. Other tasks they can do at that time to make the following day more efficient are sharpening their pencils, packing their snacks and lunches, and having their papers signed.

Although it may not be easy to have children milling around you while they perform these tasks, it is probably better than finding out the next morning that they need to write a paragraph, ten minutes before the bus is due.

Keep a checklist of these preparation jobs posted in the kitchen and award prizes at the end of the week if your children are organized.

2. Don't nag the kids about homework. Get a loud kitchen timer. The ticking will remind them to finish their work before the timer rings.

3. Let the kids help you cook. This will probably delay the process, but it will give you more time with your children and will foster closeness. Assign them specific jobs tailored to their ages, such as choosing and preparing side dishes. You will find that they eat better too.

You can encourage this practice by giving a child with culinary leanings her own recipe box. Each time she learns to prepare a new dish, she can add the recipe to her box. As the collection grows, she will feel a tremendous sense of accomplishment knowing that she can prepare so many foods on her own.

Some women also suggested a one-on-one approach, choosing a different child each night to help with the meal preparation. This provides precious private time for each child and a forum in which he or she can air the events and feelings of the day.

4. Have an older child read to a younger child. One mother invested in stickers and prizes so that her daughter could open up her own "school." Each day she teaches the *Aleph-Beis* to her younger siblings and cousin, and awards them prizes for doing well.

Exercise: Inspirational Decorating

When it's hard to keep going and you think you'll explode, the advertisers tell you to reach for a Coke or a cookie. If your waistline can't afford all those cookies, why not reach for a little inspiration instead?

We have practiced collecting positive thoughts a few times in the book. In the learning chapter we collected Torah concepts and in the morning chapter we collected grateful thoughts. This time we are looking for humorous and energizing thoughts or for a saying that helps us look at our problem from a lighter perspective.

Begin by collecting clippings, sayings, cartoons, and photographs that bring a smile to your face. Then tape your new decorations in strategic places in the kitchen, where you are likely to see them at the most hectic times. Your new hangings do not have to cause clutter. If you like organization or you are artistically inclined, you might consider mounting your exhibits neatly, or even setting aside one wall of the kitchen for display. The important thing is that the uplifting thoughts you need will be right at hand during rush hour.

True Responses: Inspirational Decorating

Here are some of the workshop participants' favorite tack-up sayings, and the thoughts behind them.

1. **You don't have too much in your house. You just have a lot in your house.**

When I was in school in Israel, my roommate volunteered to help a family with pre-Pesach preparations. One of their children had volunteered to run a "day camp" for all the neighboring families so that the other mothers could clean for Pesach calmly. There were many children in that small kitchen. One of the family's children said to the mother, "There are just too many kids in here!"

The mother replied, "Thank God there are not too many — there are just a lot!"

2. "My child, you are blessed."

I'm a grandmother myself now, but I remember that when I was raising my little ones, I frequently complained to my mother. "Mother, I just don't have the strength," I would tell her. "My child, you are blessed," she would say. She was right. It's important to remember that the little people who cause headaches are the blessings in themselves.

3. "It's better to start earlier and go slowly and steadily."

We often get into trouble because we procrastinate. When I was a girl, I learned a French saying taken from the title of one of Aesop's fables, "The Tortoise and the Hare." Do you remember that story? When I find myself running around like a hare trying to catch up, I tell myself, "Take a lesson from this story. It's better to start earlier and work slowly and steadily."

4. "What you are complaining about is what someone else is praying for."

My friend and I both hit thirty-eight this past month. We're barely in touch anymore because we live in different states, but she called yesterday to say hello. I'm the mother of three beautiful children, the oldest of whom is three and a half. They often take my breath away. I didn't expect mothering to be that challenging. My friend, unfortunately, has been trying every possible therapy, yet has not been blessed with a child. She had to take injections daily, write up charts, and take endless tests, but nothing has worked. As I spoke to her, I felt I had an embarrassment of riches.

5. **"All the dirty dishes on a scale."**

Every Saturday night my sisters and I have a conference call with our mother. We choose one character trait each week that we will work on. Last week's goal was doing kind acts. My mother commented, "Our Sages say that every kind act we do, no matter how mundane, is remembered by Hashem. Imagine when we get to the next world how heavy our scale of good deeds will be! It will be weighed down with all the pots, baking pans, and dishes from all the meals that we've served in our lives."

6. **Thank God for dirty dishes,**
   They have their tales to tell:
   While other folks go hungry,
   We're eating very well.

There I was in the supermarket parking lot, wheeling a big wagon piled up with groceries. A woman passed by and said with a smile, "Wait — the worst is yet to come!" I replied, "Thank God I'm able to afford it," thinking of my recent trip to Israel where I had met many people who really could not buy food so freely. I also thought of the Jews in Russia, who *have* no food to buy.

The woman looked right into my eyes. "You are so right," she said softly.

A Little Inner Joy Goes a Long Way

━━━ Practical Tips for Rush Hour ━━━

1. Simplify! One reason we feel the pressure mounting is that we allow many extraneous demands to intrude on this very precious time.

a. Don't talk on the phone during rush hour unless it's an emergency. It's a time when you can't really talk and you can't truly listen. Accidents frequently take place in the home at hectic times when the mother isn't looking.

b. Resist sorting your mail. You probably won't be able to take care of it and will most likely misplace things. Keep all the mail in a drawer and set aside a calmer time to sort it.

c. Make it clear to your neighbor that once your children come home, you can't run up to her even for "just a few minutes."

2. Constantly repeat to yourself: "No matter what happens, I'm going to look ahead and do the next task, and not backward to what I should have done earlier."

3. Plan ahead for rush hour. Here are some ideas:

a. Make a checklist of things you always need for the evening meal.

b. Aim to prepare supper in the morning two days a week.

c. Cut up fruit and melon in handy portions as a snack for the kids when they come home.

d. A cutlery basket is handy for a youngster who is helping you set the table.

e. When cooking early in the week, peel extra vegetables and have them ready in the fridge. The following evening's side dish or soup can be ready on demand.

f. Clean the chicken ahead of time and arrange it in the pan with the spices.

g. Some foods such as rice can be cooked ahead and can accompany more than one meal.

Chapter 12
Mealtime

Malya said, "I'm always at work. I'm serving food to others in some form twenty-four hours a day, seven days a week, 365 days a year."

Her feeling was quickly echoed by the other women in the workshop. There was no one who did not have strong feelings on this topic!

"I love my children," Rivka said, "but I feel that I can never get anything done. My three-year-old, two-year-old, and infant are constantly asking for food. It's an endless cycle of cooking, serving, and cleaning up."

Pessy laughed. "If only they would eat what we serve! When you make a peanut butter sandwich, they say they wanted cream cheese."

Kaila added, "That's not all. How about when I prepare a three-course chicken dinner and they ask for peanut butter sandwiches instead."

"You haven't even touched on the incidental aspect of mealtime," Malky commented. "The drinks that spill, the quarreling over who got a bigger portion, the child who refuses to eat his burger because the ketchup from the French fries touched it and he likes ketchup only with French fries but not with meat — or when the doorbell rings in the middle of supper and they all run to the door and return ten minutes later to ask you to rewarm everything."

Yaffa said, "Cleaning up is a hassle, even if the child can't be blamed. This morning my one-year-old took his bowl of cereal, turned it over, and put it on his head. He's only a baby, but you never get done."

Wouldn't it be nice if our children behaved perfectly during meals and loved the foods that were good for them? Can you imagine them asking for string beans instead of chocolate cake? The reality is that it's hard to get our families to sit in one place until the meal is finished, and even harder to get them to eat nutritious food once they are at the table. At each meal, there is a different kind of pressure. Breakfast is never relaxed; we are worried about getting everyone packed and on their way quickly. Catching the bus becomes more important than eating a healthy breakfast. Lunch means interrupting our work to set up and serve and clear off. At dinner time we feel droopy, and the demands seem to pour in from all sides. Certainly you know what it feels like to survey a dinner table that needs to be cleared off at 7:30. You think: "I feel helpless. I just never catch up, never get a rest, and my head hurts. I know I should be everything charming to my family, but what I really want to do is lock the door and go to sleep."

These are just some of the many problems mothers have to deal with at mealtime. When I took a survey and asked women what needed fixing about mealtimes, many of them simply replied, "Everything!" Mealtime is a routine that has rusted over the years in many homes. We wish our tables weren't so quarrelsome and disorganized and that the family would eat together at regular times, but it seems too hard to try and repair a damaged pattern.

Here is a smorgasbord (no pun intended) of suggestions for quality mealtimes from workshop participants. Each one is valuable, but please don't decide to implement them all immediately. If you want to see impressive results, start with just one or two of these ideas and aim for one transformed weeknight dinner. Gradual changes last longer.

Scheduling

Tova Gitel said, "I spoke with Dr. Yisroel Abuchatzeira. He said that American eating habits cause serious harm to our systems. From a young age we are raised with around-the-clock eating, and our bodies develop a need to snack constantly. I knew he was right, because I always had a cup of coffee in my hand and I was always hungry. He said, 'One should eat three times a day and never snack. Children should develop proper eating rhythms from a very young age.' "

How can we prevent the problem of around-the-clock eating and serving? The first step is to stop skipping meals yourself and then trying to catch up by snacking. When you skip a meal, your child sees what you are doing and learns that not eating on a schedule is okay. Second, plan a schedule for all three meals for the coming week, and stick to it. This will help you establish the new routine of eating balanced meals at the same time each day. Tell your family that you will not be serving in-between meals. Third, if you must offer snacks, minimize the options. Offer foods that are healthy and ones that a child can take for himself.

You may be smiling as you read this and thinking, "This is not me. I could never change my household around." Allow me to share Tova's final, encouraging statement: "Once I began eating healthfully, I suddenly found that I no longer had the stomach problems that had been a part of my life for so many years. I really felt better! I was totally blown away. It may seem hard at first to set up a routine, but if you are convinced that it will be much better for everyone in your house, you'll have the inner conviction to push it through."

Eating Habits

Baila said, "I'm trying to change my family's eating habits. I bought several new cookbooks, and I've decided to serve whole grains, beans and vegetables that aren't canned or processed. The transition has certainly been interesting! Last night my three-year-old daughter looked at her plate and exclaimed, 'What is *this*?' She didn't recognize any of the foods. My husband dug out an old encyclopedia. He found pictures of all the grains and beans growing, and explained how Hashem takes care of every plant so that we can have food. She tasted her supper and then ate all of it. Today while she helped me sort and check the beans she said, 'Does Hashem make *this* food for us too?' She was amazed at the variety of edible items that she had never seen before!"

Baila offered two tips for changing children's attitudes about healthy food and breaking down their resistance to a menu that isn't loaded with sugar and chemicals. She suggests first of all that you get them interested by explaining on their level how and where the food originates and what it does in their bodies, and by letting them help you prepare parts of the meal. Secondly, you might also try to encourage your child whenever you catch him with a mouthful. Say, "I'm glad you are enjoying the salad" or "I'm happy you like the corn macaroni we have today." This will show him that cooperating at mealtime has an added bonus: attention.

It's also helpful to gear the appropriate amounts and types of food to your child's age and size. Have a realistic picture of what he can eat and adjust the portions accordingly. Some kids are so overwhelmed when they see a large portion that they don't even touch it. You can also relax and feel secure about the meal itself. A diet which consists mainly of grains, salads, vegetable soup, and fresh fruit may sound alarming to you, but a nutritionist will probably tell you that it is exactly what your child needs. Many kids are allergic to milk and dairy products, and less sugar will reduce hyperactivity. So good eating habits not only benefit your kids, they benefit you as well.

Quality Time

Regulating mealtime schedules and encouraging good eating habits can go a long way toward a calmer and healthier atmosphere at the dinner table. But we can go even further to enhance our meals. This means not just eliminating negative patterns, but making mealtime a quality time. Our Sages said: כָּל זְמַן שֶׁבֵּית הַמִקְדָש קַיָם מִזְבֵּחַ מְכַפֵּר עַל יִשְׂרָאֵל, וְעַכְשָׁיו שֻׁלְחָנוֹ שֶׁל אָדָם מְכַפֵּר *As long as we had the Holy Temple, the Altar atoned for our sins. Now, one's table atones for his sins* (*Berachos* 55).

We might be familiar with the concept of שֻׁלְחָן דוֹמֶה לְמִזְבֵּחַ, *the table is like* (in place of) *the Altar.* But we never really think about the implications when we sit down to eat. Try to picture what took place in the *Beis Hamikdash:* When a sacrifice was brought for Hashem on the Altar, a fire descended from the sky in the shape of a flaming lion, and consumed it. The Levites sang and played musical instruments, and representatives of all the tribes of Israel said special prayers. It was an event of indescribable holiness.

Our table is compared to this Altar in two ways. One type of sacrifice atoned for sins. The *todah* sacrifice expressed gratitude, while *olah* sacrifices were in appreciation for enabling one to do *mitzvos.* These *korbanos* showed the Jew's yearning to rise closer to Hashem. Our dinner table today is meant to serve the same purposes. In *The Foundation of Repentance,* Rabbeinu Yonah of Gerona (1180-1263) suggests that at our table we should review our deeds, both good and bad; we should regret our misdeeds, but remember at the same time the *mitzvos* we have done and be thankful for every short interval of living righteously. He says:

> This is the path in which one should go and the deed that he should do to habituate himself to guard against any sin. In the morning when he awakes

from his sleep, he should have in mind that he will
repent and examine his deeds, and that . . . he will
not pervert even one footstep. At mealtime, before he
eats, he should confess all his sins . . .

If mealtime comes and one searches and has not
found abominations, then let him thank and give
praise before his Creator for having helped him
against his enemies, and for having been privileged
to spend an hour of repentance in this world. Then
let him eat his morning meal; and before his evening
meal let him confess everything, as we have said.
And so let him do from the time of his evening meal
until bedtime.

This passage demonstrates Rabbeinu Yonah's awareness
— about seven hundred and fifty years ago — of the importance of positive reinforcement. A modern-day psychologist
will tell you that when you see a person doing something well,
even if it is something small or of short duration, praise him
and reinforce the behavior with positive feedback. Rabbeinu
Yonah does the same thing; he tells us to acquire the habit of
recalling the triumphs in our efforts to change for the better,
at regular intervals each day. One who does this before eating
elevates the entire meal.

Henya described how she has taken this lofty insight and
turned it into a part of her family's routine. "My husband and
I have everyone, including ourselves, take a turn talking about
a *mitzvah* they did that day. The children really gain from sharing their moments of triumph. The conversation also generates ideas for good things the kids can plan to do the next
day."

Another way in which we can elevate our meals is by maintaining the holy, serene atmosphere that existed in the *Beis
Hamikdash*. We can turn this ideal into a reality by making
the table a place where Torah learning, appropriate blessings,
and kindness to others takes place.

Sima said, "Don't most of the fights at the table start when you are on the phone? The first step is to make a rule: no telephone interruptions. Someone in Montreal once asked the Rosh Yeshiva how to improve the *chinuch* of his children. The Rosh Yeshiva said, 'Take time to be with your children and talk to them during meals. I will take calls at any time during the day, but I refuse telephone interruptions during meals.' "

Yael said, "I asked Rav Bik, *shlita,* what we can do to instill sincerity and exemplary *midos* in our children. His answer also had to do with meals. He said, 'Never talk *loshon hara* at your table. Specifically, don't disparage Jewish groups or gossip about religious people who were caught doing something wrong. Your intention might be to show that you are more righteous than someone else and that your way is better. Your child, however, learns to be cynical of everyone.' "

Discussing a Torah idea, even briefly, or asking the kids to tell you something they learned in *Chumash* that day can also help to create the proper atmosphere at the table.

Company

Our Sages say, הַמַּאֲרִיךְ עַל שֻׁלְחָנוֹ מַאֲרִיכִין לוֹ יָמָיו וּשְׁנוֹתָיו, *One who extends one's table will merit a longer life* (*Berachos,* 54:2). This doesn't mean adding a leaf to the dining room table. What does it mean?

On a practical level, "extending" may mean that if you eat slowly and calmly, you will be healthier and live longer. It can also mean that you should prolong the meal with Torah thoughts. Most importantly, it means extending yourself to others; through your generosity, others can also enjoy a meal. This happens when you prepare a meal to deliver to someone, or give charity before you eat. Of course, our main "extension" is having guests, and company benefits us as much as it does the guest.

Chaya said, "I've noticed that when we have guests at the table, everyone is on their best behavior. We have a very lively and friendly neighbor who happens to live alone. She comes quite often to visit and enjoy the children during the week. When she joins us for supper, she likes to bring the dessert. Whenever she thanks me for inviting her, I reply, 'You are doing us such a favor! You always bring out the best in everyone.' "

Tamar said, "We can't have the ideal supper every night. On some nights everyone eats at a different time because each one has his own plans; one eats before play practice, and the other eats late after a long evening session of learning. However, every Wednesday night everyone in the family knows that they must be home on time for supper, because Wednesday night is when *Zeide* comes to eat with us. The children tell him what they learned in school and show him their test papers or projects. He tells stories and asks Torah riddles, answers their questions on homework, and holds the baby and plays with her."

One last important tip: even without company, it is very important for a family to eat the main meal together. If this is simply not realistic in your household, try to eat together at least once or twice during the week. Many families are so rushed and pressured by the multiple demands of daily life that the only time the members see each other is on Shabbos. The result is a sad fragmentation of the family unit. Eating together reinforces closeness and gives parents and children — and siblings — a chance to get to know each other better.

Exercise: Making Mealtime Quality Time

If everyone is busy talking about something constructive at the table, the meal will not be consumed by squabbles and bickering. The important guideline to enforce is that every person takes one turn and says only one thing. You don't want the older children taking up the conversation while the younger ones feel frustrated because they can't think of anything to add.

What creative topics for discussion can you incorporate into your meal?

_____

_____

_____

True Responses: Making Mealtime Quality Time

1. At the dinner table in our house each person talks about something he learned and the person it was learned from. One day, when it was my turn, I said, "I *davened Minchah* today, even though I often forget. I learned this from Chavy. She told me that she started *davening Minchah* in school during her afternoon recess. Her classmates followed her example, and the teacher gave them all extra free time."

2. We have story night once a week. Everyone gets to tell a story. The older children will read from a book they like, such as the "Maggid" series by Paysach Krohn or the books by Hanoch Teller. The younger ones invent their own stories. Once in a while the stories the younger children invent are the most interesting ones.

3. My daughter told me that in Pre-1-A they have a "Good News" routine every morning, with each child making a personal contribution. I liked this idea, so we started taking turns telling our good news at the meal at night.

4. We have a unique centerpiece each night: a display of each family member's favorite object of the day. Everyone puts something at the center of the table and gets to talk about it during the meal. It could be a test paper or a letter that came in the mail or a sticker someone got from the teacher.

5. Sometimes we have everyone take a turn telling about something they learned. The children repeat what they learned in school, and I relate what I learned from a *sefer* or from Dial-A-Shiur. (Just between us, I've had several emergencies where I had to call my uncle for something to say at the last minute!)

Here is a game that I sometimes play with my children at dinnertime. It's not only a good diversion but fosters appreciation too. It's called:

Looking At Your House With Different Glasses

1. Look around your home. Record three defects you notice in your environment, like the scratches on the furniture, the three-inch pile of unsorted mail, or the nick the doorknob made in the wall.

_____

_____

_____

_____

2. Now take another look. Record the things around you that are pleasant, comfortable, relaxing, helpful, in good taste, cozy, colorful, and neat. Here is the challenge: for every one negative thing you wrote you now have to think of two positive things. Of course, you can always add more.

_____

_____

_____

_____

_____

_____

_____

_____

A Little Inner Joy Goes a Long Way

Practical Tips for a Calmer Meal

1. Plan a specific schedule for each meal, including breakfast. To whatever extent possible, get the members of your family to adhere to the schedule.

2. Make your children active participants in the meal. Let them prepare part of it or at least set the table. Have a "scientific" discussion about the food itself — its origin and nutritional value.

3. When quarrels occur, put them on hold. Tell the parties that they may continue the argument after supper, but that the meal must remain undisturbed.

4. Invite a guest. Having company once a week or twice a month on weeknights brings out the best in all of us.

5. Guide the conversation around constructive topics, so that everyone will remain comfortable and cheerful.

6. Try to remain calm during the meal. When the mother is calm, everyone else tends to relax as well.

7. Set a nice table, even if you are only using paper products. A neat, laid-out table with a bread basket (and maybe even flowers) makes the meal more appetizing.

Chapter 13
Nighttime

Darkness had come several hours earlier, and now I was snuggling up with my son before tucking him under his fluffy comforter. The past few nights had been interrupted by the eerie sounds of air-raid sirens. The war in the Persian Gulf and the Scud missile attacks had altered our bedtime rituals. The night was now filled with frightening and awesome technology that brought messages of destruction and death in its wake. So tonight I lingered as I eased him into sleep.

As I was saying goodnight, Shooie turned to me, his eyes filled with sincerity and curiosity, and asked in a gentle voice, "Mommy, how long is the night?"

I was caught off guard by this question from my sensitive four-year-old. I found myself answering,

"Not too long, Shooie, not too long." (*How Long The Night*, Mindy Gross)

How long is the night? We have all had times when we gazed at the clock and asked this question. Nighttime is a potentially stressful time. Not the least of the frustrations that we may experience is insomnia. When we can't sleep, we don't know what to do with ourselves. We don't want to wake others, but straining to relax only makes us feel more restless. The thought that drums inside our heads is that we *must* get some sleep or we'll walk around all day tomorrow in a fog.

While we lie awake at night, we are plagued by our worries. Loneliness and pain are felt more potently at night because there are fewer diversions. It's at night that your backache acts up and your sore tooth throbs. *Chazal* say that a person who is sick feels worse at night. And insomnia can aggravate any of these troubles.

Sleep is so delicate. It flies away easily. The slightest noise, be it a dripping faucet or rain pattering on your roof, can throw your sense of rhythm off. If someone sleeping near you has a cold, his or her labored breathing may be enough to drive you crazy. Most of us live in very noisy surroundings; there are car alarms going off, telephones ringing, police or ambulance sirens wailing, and loud music echoing on the streets. Yet on a quiet night, one small sound is enough to tick you off. And once your sleep is disturbed, you may not fall asleep again until the wee hours of the morning. You were dozing off during the day and now when you have the opportunity to sleep, nothing seems to work.

We are all very concerned about getting an adequate amount of rest. The *Rambam* says that ideally we should sleep for eight hours each night, an elusive goal for most people. But at the same time, we know that without a good night's sleep we won't feel alert during the day and we won't be able to make full use of our abilities.

What can we do to prevent the unnecessary waste of these precious nighttime hours? The remedy is right at hand.

When you can't sleep at night, speak to Hashem.

In *Chovos Halevavos*, we find the following benefits of praying to Hashem at night:

> 1. *One has more time.*
> 2. *One is not as hungry at night as during the day, so he can concentrate better.*
> 3. *There are fewer interruptions. Friends don't come to visit, and creditors don't bang on the door. There are fewer distractions and less noise.*
> 4. *One has more privacy.*

The author reminds us of some great people who found solace in speaking to Hashem at night. One of them was King David, who mentions his nighttime communication with Hashem in several places in *Tehillim*: "At night I remembered You, Hashem" (119:55); "I awoke at midnight to thank You" (119:62); "The time I called out to You was at night" (88:2). David's son Shlomo writes in the same vein in *Shir Hashirim*: "When I lay down at night, I sought the One my soul loves" (3:1).

What prayers should one say at night if he has trouble sleeping? The chapters of *Tehillim* that the *Chovos HaLevavos* recommends to be said at night are chapters 119 and all fifteen of the *Shir Hama'alos* (120-134).

However, there is one other very obvious prayer one can say at night. We may have known this truth for years and then forgotten it, because the habit of repeating the same prayer over and over erodes its significance.

Some nights you feel so tired that you can't think or see straight; just sitting up takes concentrated effort. If you've neglected to keep a *siddur* at hand it is so tempting to say the *Shema* quickly by heart. And there are some nights when you don't say it altogether. You might have decided to rest just a little after you put the children to bed. It's too early to think of saying *Shema*, yet it feels so good to stretch out that you fall asleep, and the next time you wake up, it is dawn. On those nights when you do manage to say *Shema* from a *siddur*, the words run together, and you find once again that you have mumbled the prayer mechanically, without concentrating on each individual word.

Yet the bedtime *Shema* is a precious treasure — and not only for insomnia. Before we go to sleep, we ask Hashem to send the angels to watch over us. They protect us from physical harm and illness and from emotional trauma. We also ask Hashem that we not be frightened by bad dreams.

I once knew that saying the bedtime *Shema* was the key to a good night's sleep. Yet over the years I had forgotten. I discovered the security the *Shema* had once given me as a child during a conversation with my young daughter. My parents had just returned from a trip and called to say they were home. The next day I went to visit them, taking along my four-year-old daughter, Chaya Rivky. I had a long conversation with my mother in which I told her all the things you never quite say when you are talking long-distance. At first my daughter sat patiently, but after a while she grew restless. She asked me if I would take her up to see the doll collection in my old room. We went upstairs and Chaya Rivky was full of questions about the nighttimes of my childhood:

"Mommy, did you really sleep in this little bed? Where did Aunt Manya sleep? Why didn't both of you share a room, like I share my room with Chavie? Shulem sleeps in his own room and he always says, 'I'm scared.' Were *you* scared?"

My daughter's questions sent a shower of nostalgia over me. I still remember how my face had lit up when my mother opened the door and showed me my new bed — the first bed I ever slept in. I ran around it, examining it from all sides and thinking how grown-up it felt to have a big bed in my own room.

From the time I was three, I had slept alone in that room. It was a small room, with a small closet and dresser against the wall. My doll collection sat on top of the dresser. I loved the picture of the cherry tree that hung over my bed; my mother had needlepointed it many years before I was born. On the night table there was a small night-light with a music box inside that played a lullaby when you wound the key. The room was so pleasant, but of course there were times when I had been scared at night.

I smiled as I looked at Chaya Rivky and said, "Yes, sometimes I was scared sleeping all alone."

Chaya Rivky stared at me. She just couldn't imagine her mommy being scared at night. "Did you run to *Bobby* or *Zeide's* bed when you got scared?" she asked.

"When I was your age I did, but then one day my mother said, 'You are a big girl already. You shouldn't wake up *Tatty* or Mommy anymore when they are sleeping.' "

"Did you go to your sister's bed and wake her up?" Chaya Rivky asked.

"Not exactly," I laughed. "But my big sister Manya helped me in a different way." Then I told her a story that I hadn't thought about in a long, long time.

It happened the winter before Manya got married, so I must have been about six-years-old. We had visitors from England, and my older sister moved into my room and slept with me for about a week. I was so happy to share my room; it felt good to have her nearby and not to sleep alone at night. I noticed that each night before she went to sleep, she said something from the *siddur*. "What are you saying, Manya?" I asked.

"Before we go to sleep, we say *Shema* and ask Hashem to send the *malachim* to watch over us. They protect us from all sides," my sister replied.

"Manya, I only say the first part of the *Shema*," I told her. "I don't say the part about the *malachim* watching us. Can you say that part with me? Sometimes I'm scared at night."

Manya agreed and said the entire bedtime *Shema* with me. "If you are scared, just remember that the angels are protecting you," she reminded me.

A week later Manya moved back to her room, and I was all alone again. I didn't realize until I was already in bed that she hadn't said *Shema* with me, and I was sure that I just couldn't go to sleep without those prayers. I heard my parents talking to each other from the doorway and called out, *"Tatty,* last night Manya said the whole *Shema* with me, and I slept so well. Could you say it with me tonight?"

For about two years, my father said *Shema* out loud with me every night, word by word. He pronounced the words in his heavy Galician accent, and I repeated after him as best I could. I always fell asleep with a happy, secure feeling.

I sat quietly next to Chaya Rivky and listened to my heart, where I heard the echo of my father's fervent, calm, and trusting voice. I realized that back then, as a young child, I had known his faith; it was contained in those words of the *Shema*. I might not have been able to explain such faith as a six-year-old, but I understood that it surrounded me like a protective cushion. Now, as an adult, I could explain it adequately — but could I *feel* it? Could I feel the security that my father's *bitachon* had given me each night? Could I give my child that feeling? I felt it was a worthwhile idea to work on.

It is interesting how the spiritual concerns that weigh on our hearts are supported from Above. When we are thinking sincerely about our service of Hashem, we often receive encouragement and guidance in the least expected ways.

Not long after that talk with my daughter, I decided to clean out the drawer where I keep my Torah tapes. What a mess! There were at least 200 tapes in there, most labeled with only a number. How would I ever get them organized? I decided to take out four tapes at random and listen to a five-minute segment of each one. At least I would get some idea what the topics were.

The fourth tape was on *Ein Yaakov*, by Rabbi Fishel Shachter. When I pressed the "play" button, Rabbi Shachter was saying . . . "And this portion of the *Gemara* teaches us that saying the bedtime *Shema* can make the difference between a scary dream and a happy dream." What a marvelous gift! Hashem knew that the *Shema* was on my mind, and He had sent me more information about it. Now I not only knew that *Shema* was a good cure for insomnia and a pledge of faith, but also that it could affect our dreams positively.

Rabbi Shachter mentioned yet another benefit of the *Shema*: It is a protection for the body.

> "There are two hundred and forty-eight words in the *Shema*. There are two hundred and forty-eight limbs in our bodies. The words of the *Shema* are intended to protect all of our limbs.
>
> One who reads the *Shema* properly and pronounces each word carefully and with concentration causes holiness to dwell on each of his limbs. If he doesn't say the *Shema* with concentration, if he hurries, and his heart is pondering other things and he doesn't know what his mouth says, then every limb is controlled by other forces. And God forbid, there will come upon people illnesses and pain, because they are not careful to concentrate when they say the *Shema*." *(Sefer Kav Hayosher, chapter 51)*

What a tremendous fortune we have been given! A single prayer that can help us in so many ways. It really is worth the extra effort we will have to put in at night to say the *Shema* with concentration. The dividends can be priceless.

On the flip side of insomnia, the times when you simply can't fall asleep, is another major harassment of the night: being awakened.

Our leaders have always been extremely sensitive to the basic human need for a good night's rest. Their motto has been: Don't do unto others what you would not want done to you. The *Chofetz Chaim* commented that robbing a person of sleep is worse than robbing money, for money can be returned, while sleep cannot. There are many stories of *gedolim* who went out of their way to assure those around them a peaceful slumber.

A young man was once a guest at the *Chazon Ish's* home. The guest bed was in the room where the *Chazon Ish* studied, and although the guest insisted that even ten lamps would not bother him, the *Chazon Ish* extinguished the lamp and went to sleep earlier than usual to enable the guest to get a good night's rest. The *Chazon Ish's* diligence in Torah study was renowned, and yet he renounced it for an act which he considered more important at the time (*P'eir HaDor*, Biography of the *Chazon Ish*).

Whenever Rabbi Yisroel Salanter saw a broken window shutter, he would fix it, even if the owner was a complete stranger. He did not want the shutter to bang at night and thereby rouse people from their sleep (*Tnuas HaMussar*, Vol. 1).

Someone once asked Rabbi Yosef Chaim Sonnenfeld, the rabbi of Jerusalem, if it was permissible to have a hot drink before the morning prayers. Rabbi Sonnenfeld replied affirmatively. An acquaintance of Rabbi Sonnenfeld who overheard this discussion asked him, "But Rabbi, don't you refrain from having a hot drink before morning prayers?"

"You are right," replied Rav Yosef Chaim, "but I do so for a special reason. I'm afraid that if I make it known that I would like a hot drink before morning prayers, my wife might wake up early in the morning to warm the water for me." (*Morah D'Arah B'Yisroel,* vol. 1). [Love Your Neighbor, pp. 249, 250]

Assuring another person's rest is a big *mitzvah.* The problem is that it is much more difficult to assure our own. We may be lucky enough not to suffer from insomnia, but will we ever have children who always sleep through the night? Mothers are on call twenty-four hours a day, and it is then that our *middos* are really put to the test.

I got a call several weeks ago to volunteer to guard my speech for two hours a day for the merit of someone who is seriously ill. I offered two daytime hours and then graciously added, "I'll take the hours from twelve to six a.m. too."

My friend asked, "Are you sure? Remember, I mentioned that we are not only avoiding slander, but also words of anger. If someone wakes you up at two a.m., are you sure you'll remain calm?"

The silence at my end was her answer. We decided we would both take the night hours so that if one of us slipped, the other would back her up.

We are all much more prone to grouchiness at two a.m. A voice in us insists that being deprived of sleep is simply unfair. Despite what all the developmental books say, the mothers I know agree that the average child will wake you up at night until he is about eighteen months old. Add to that the challenge of having more than one toddler, and you have the potential for a very interesting situation.

The best perspective I can offer you on how to cope with being awakened by children is the advice of Chedva Silverfarb, the young woman of valor from Israel who died tragically of a fatal illness at the age of twenty-seven. Chedva wrote these words when she had come to America for treatment:

> When I returned to school after the birth of my third child, I complained to some of the teachers that I constantly felt tired. Bone weary. I had not gotten a decent night's sleep in three years, since the birth of my oldest child. Every night the children would wake me up, one by one. I would wind up roaming around the house throughout the night, tending to their needs.
>
> Since I've come to America, I have not slept through the night. I toss and turn in my bed, staring at the clock which seems to stand still. I literally feel the meaning of the pasuk, "In the morning you will await evening and in the evening you will await morning" on my body.
>
> Now it is not my children who disturb my sleep. My room is as quiet as can be. No one disturbs me. In the middle of a sleepless night I think to myself: Ribono Shel Olam, if only You will give me the zechus to return to my home and to my children, I will do what comes naturally to all mothers. I will care for them. And when they wake me in the middle of the

night, I won't walk into their room to take care of them. Ribono Shel Olam, I will dance over to their beds.

Boruch Hashem, I did return to my family in Eretz Yisrael. And every time I woke up in the middle of the night to care for my children, I felt as if my heart were bursting with joy. I was so happy that I felt like turning on a music tape and dancing. (*A Narrow Bridge,* by D. Dubinki)

No one should ever need a serious illness, God forbid, in order to appreciate her family, but the principle is the best one around. It means that even at two a.m. we have to count our blessings, and if we do, we will be amazed at the therapeutic results.

Sometimes, however it is not children that disturb our sleep, but worries which may indeed be very real. Fatigue makes us vulnerable to anxiety, and nighttime is when our concerns seem to attack with the most force. As Miriam Adahan comments so aptly in *Raising Children to Care*: "When you are tired, you are most apt to make mountains out of molehills and have pessimistic thoughts about yourself and your life."

We have to be careful not to fall into the anxiety whirlpool. Every problem that occurs during the day can turn into a major crisis when we toss it around in our heads at night. An embarrassing situation that lasted five minutes can keep us up for an hour, thinking about how everyone will see us as a loser from now on. If someone upset us, we blame ourselves and think of ten different things we *could* have said, but didn't think of in time. If a precious item broke or a project fell through, we tend to think that we are simply incompetent. At night, our entire future seems to hinge on that one bad thing that happened during the day, and we feel sucked into the grasp of painful scenarios and morbid expectations.

This magnified whirlpool cycle isn't accurate. If we looked at the total picture in a more objective light, we would find the hopeful side to these problems. However, at night, when we are exhausted, it's hard to be fair to ourselves. The thoughts we want to escape are stronger than usual, and we need to work consciously to climb out of their grip. We may know inside that the reality is not as bleak as our nighttime picture, but we can't figure out how to unload the worries. Who has the strength to think effectively at night?

It's important to remember the Jewish tradition that the day begins with the preceding evening. Shabbos and holidays begin in the evening. We have to unload the past at night and prepare for a new and better genesis.

Here is an exercise that can help you shake off part of your burden and go to sleep peacefully at night. It will help you differentiate between your serious and less serious worries. This may seem overwhelming, but it is actually an uncomplicated selection process. You will be telling yourself things that you wouldn't want someone else to tell you, but when you find it out for yourself, you will gently grow.

Exercise: Prioritizing Worries

1. Make a list of eight worries that are bothering you right now. I know you have some major concerns, but for this exercise choose only things that you know can be resolved this week.
2. Prepare eight index cards or strips of paper and copy one worry on to each card.
3. Sort them in order of priority. Which worry bothers you the most? Put it in front, and the others behind it in descending order.
4. On a sheet of paper, write down the two most important worries.
5. On the other side of the sheet write down a personal prayer to Hashem or some verses from *Tehillim* that would apply to your worry. Put this sheet in your *siddur*.
6. Take all your index cards or small slips of paper and throw them away.

7. Say the verse, הַשְׁלֵךְ עַל ה׳ יְהָבְךָ וְהוּא יְכַלְכְּלֶךָ, *Throw the weight of your worries onto Hashem, and He will sustain you* (*Tehillim* 55:23).

Writing things down serves two wonderful purposes. It releases the worry from inside you and transfers it to a piece of paper, where it doesn't seem quite so intense. And it makes you feel that you have begun to do something about the problem, so there is less to worry about.

The seventh step in the exercise is very important. When it comes to the really important concerns, we can make our lives so much easier by "throwing the weight" onto Hashem, Who can surely support it.

The *Chofetz Chaim* tells the story of a poor peddler who was walking and carrying a heavy bundle. A kindhearted magnate passed by in an elegant coach and offered the pauper a ride. The pauper accepted and sat in the carriage holding his bundle.

"Why don't you put your heavy bundle down?" the magnate asked.

"I don't want to impose," said the pauper. "It's enough that you are transporting me; I don't want you to have to carry my bundle as well."

Hashem provides for every breath of our lives and supervises the welfare of the entire universe. Why do we hold on tightly to our personal bundle of worries? Are we afraid that He can't hold it for us? Throw away your minor worries, and give the major ones to God.

True Responses: Prioritizing Worries

The responses to this exercise in the workshop elicited some startling and very humorous discoveries about the women's thinking patterns. As we worked on prioritizing our worries, Mirel said, "I can't do this. How can I decide which worries are most important? Everything I worry about is important."

Etty suggested, "Put the problems that you will have to deal with sooner before the ones that come later."

Mirel said, "Maybe I won't have time to worry about them later!" She paused and laughed. "Did I say that? I sound like I enjoy worrying."

I sympathized with Mirel. "We are so used to troubling ourselves with anxious thoughts all day that we don't even realize what we are doing. We don't realize the energy these thoughts are consuming. Although it's just a triviality, at that time it is on our minds, and it robs us of the quality of life. That's why I wanted us to try to write the worries down, and learn to pray about them instead."

Necha said, " I don't have any worries to write about, even for the sake of the conversation. I don't worry."

Etty looked up and said wryly, "Can I be your friend?"

"It's not that simple," Mirel said. "My husband advised me to become friendly with someone who doesn't worry. Now I have to worry *for* her."

Necha offered, "Very often we worry about things but they turn out fine anyhow. I saw a cartoon about this in Dr. Twerski's book, *When Do The Good Things Start.* The little boy is sitting and looking at the A on his test paper. He sighs and says, 'Oh well, I worried how I'd do on this test all night. What a waste of a good worry!' "

Etty laughed. "My husband had to leave at five a.m. this morning on an important job. I didn't sleep all night. Every hour I checked the clock; I wanted to be sure he'd be up on time. He *did* wake up on time, but I was so tired that I slept through the ringing of the alarm clock!"

By this time everyone was laughing. We had written out our lists and were passing around the scissors, cutting them up and arranging them all over the dining room table. We decided that we would each pass up only the four most important worries to be read aloud.

Look through the following worries. Just to satisfy your own curiosity, in what order would you put each list? Do you see yourself anywhere on the page? Which worries would you discard?

As you sift, remember how important it is to get a good night's sleep.

A.

1. I worry all Friday about being ready for Shabbos.
2. I have to make a long list of phone calls for sponsors for the *tzedakah* event.
3. I always worry about getting the children ready for school in the morning. What if they miss the bus?
4. A neighbor is having surgery today. I hope it will be effective in the long run.

B.

1. I'm worried about losing weight.
2. I'm concerned about my married children's *parnasah*.
3. My daughter's teacher is strict. I hope the teacher will like her. I hope she succeeds in school.
4. I'm always misplacing things. I especially worry about losing library materials.

C.

1. I need a babysitter for this week. The last time I went out at night the babysitter couldn't manage. The house was overturned and the children didn't go to bed until I got home at 11:00 p.m.
2. My son just started in a new school. I hope he will make friends.
3. I worry about being a good example for my children.
4. I worry about not learning enough. I can never seem to find time to listen to Torah tapes or open a book.

D.

1. I am feeling very weak because of my pregnancy. The hours between five and eight o'clock at night are when I feel strongest, and I try to use that time to do the kitchen and clean up a little around the house. But I worry all day about whether I will be able to handle it.
2. I'd like to have guests for Shabbos, but I haven't cooked Shabbos for the last two weeks.
3. I'm worried that my husband's patience will wear thin because I'm able to do so little around the house lately. But that's not likely because he's very patient.

4. It's time to put away the summer clothes and take out the winter things — but I just don't have the strength for it now. I guess it all adds up to accepting the fact that I'm very tired and I can't do what I usually do. That's hard for me.

E.
1. Will my grandson's *bris* be on time?
2. Will my daughter-in-law like the robe I purchased for her?
3. I'm teaching again, and I wonder what my Pre-1-A class will be like this year.
4. I'm still looking for a babysitter for my younger child. My mother is going to pitch in for now, but I don't want that arrangement to be permanent.

F.
1. My third son is getting married and still hasn't found an apartment.
2. We need to decide which flowers we are renting for the night of the wedding.
3. At the last wedding some people felt hurt because of a triviality, although I really tried my best to smooth things over with everyone. I hope that at this wedding I can be there for all the guests.
4. This is the first time I'm having a dress sewn by a seamstress and I'm worried how it will look because she isn't that experienced.

G.
1. My closest friends are moving to Israel, and I wonder how I'll manage without them.
2. I'm starting a new job tomorrow, and I really hope it works out.
3. I'll have to wake up at 7:00 to be ready on time this year, and I've never had to do that before.
4.Whenever I put something on I notice that I have to sew on a button or fix the hem. It seems that almost everything I own is falling apart.

A Little Inner Joy Goes a Long Way

Practical Tips for Nighttime

1. Before you go to sleep, take care of one thing that will make the following day go a bit more smoothly. Lay out your clothes; pick out the recipes you want to use for supper the following night and leave them out on the counter; seal up the letter you intend to mail and put a stamp on it. You will go to sleep with a freer head, knowing you have given yourself a head start on the next day.

2. Keep Torah tapes available and listen to them if you are having trouble sleeping. Many women report that listening to Torah thoughts is very reassuring and makes them feel closer to Hashem.

3. If you are not too tired, keep a journal on your nightstand and jot down something under each of these three headings before you go to sleep:

a. Something I did right today

_____

_____

b. Something I learned today

_____

_____

c. I felt happy today when

_____

_____

4. Don't struggle against insomnia. If you decide not to fight it but to occupy yourself for a while, you will probably find that sleep comes easily.

5. Plan at least one thing for the next day that you will enjoy.

6. Use a prayer book when you say the *Shema*.

7. Say the *Shema* out loud with your children.

8. Get enough rest. To do this, you may have to relax your standards; the world will not come to an end if every last dish is not put away before you go to bed. If you find this tip difficult, use an alarm clock to remind you that it is time to go to sleep!

Chapter 14
Wrapping Up

The final step is to ask yourself what you will do once you have finished reading this book. Will you say to yourself, "Having a positive outlook is a great idea — maybe someday I'll really work on it?" Or will you take action?

Yaffa Blumenthal commented on a tape: "Why does it say וְיָדַעְתָּ הַיּוֹם וַהֲשֵׁבֹתָ אֶל לְבָבֶךְ, *You know it today; now apply it and take it to heart (Devarim 4:39)*? This teaches us that one must apply the knowledge he has learned *right away* on that day. If you postpone action, the lesson evaporates."

Most people recognize that bringing a concept to life takes work. They say they will do it tomorrow because they lack the courage, strength, and determination to do the work. They are hoping that maybe tomorrow it will be a little easier.

The power of taking immediate action was once strikingly

demonstrated to me in a story told by a lecturer.

"Two years ago," she began, "my brother decided that he wanted to quit smoking. He called me and said that he wanted to come up to my house because there were too many pressures in his own surroundings. He came up on Thursday for a long weekend. On Thursday night we all sat together telling stories and snacking on sunflower seeds. Yossi was sitting there, talking and making his plans. 'Tonight is Thursday night and tomorrow, Friday, at eleven a.m., I smoke my last cigarette,' he declared.

"My son returned from yeshiva that night and joined us at the table. My brother repeated his declaration to him: 'Tomorrow I'm quitting smoking. Tomorrow at eleven a.m. I will smoke my last cigarette. With God's help it will be my last.'

"We were sitting together. There was a bottle of Pepsi on the table and the sunflower seeds and about fifty cigarettes in the ashtray. My brother sat and puffed away. I realized that he was not thinking about tomorrow; he was just immersed in that cigarette. My son who had successfully quit smoking, said to him, 'Yossi, take that cigarette and put it out right now, and then you will know that you have quit.'

"At first Yossi made believe that he hadn't heard him. He said again, 'Yes, I know, tomorrow at eleven o'clock.'

'Yossi,' my son repeated, 'take that cigarette and put it out right now, because if you don't there will never be a tomorrow.'

"My brother panicked. There was silence in the room as he was confronted with an awesome truth. All along he'd been planning on a whole night of fun with those cigarettes. I think he had intended to stay awake and smoke five packs. He heard my son's words now, and he knew what they meant.

"I must tell you that when I saw him putting out that cigarette, I was mesmerized. I knew the power of the moment; I knew that he was doing something very precious for himself. Thank God, he hasn't smoked since."

You too can change your life, but you will need to act. A cheerful nature seldom comes by accident, and it doesn't come from outside circumstances but only from within. You now have many new ideas that can help you succeed in achieving your goal. You can encourage the cheerful side of your nature by paying attention to your thoughts, putting some energy into creating better ones, and nurturing an environment that is conducive to progress.

The rewards of being truly alive are so great that once you have tasted it you will surely want to actualize it. At a seminar, Rabbi Ezriel Tauber once challenged his audience: "Tomorrow morning when you wake up and say *Modeh Ani,* take a deep breath and thank God that you are alive." As I listened, I thought about what it would be like to wake up and feel genuinely thankful for the precious gift of life, instead of rolling over and thinking, "I wish I could be left alone." I imagined wanting to live, striving to grow and having a clear purpose in my day. I imagined always feeling that Hashem is right here, close to me. Suddenly I felt that the words *Modeh Ani* were happening to me in a deeper way than ever before. The clarity of Hashem's guidance and presence, for that instant, were suddenly so clear. I wanted to go out and shout, "I have a *neshamah* and I can feel it!" In that brief moment of revelation I had found out about the possibility of a vibrant life, and I resolved to go for it.

In the *Pele Yoaitz* on *Kinah*, the author declares, *"When we are happy, Hashem is happy.* The verse יִשְׂמַח ה׳ בְּמַעֲשָׂיו — that Hashem will rejoice when humanity obeys His command — is interpreted by the *Zohar* to mean that Hashem will rejoice when His creation is joyous. This means that we deserve to feel good. Not only that, it is a mitzvah to experience joy."

You don't have to go far. You can begin to mine the magic as soon as you put this book down. Set aside a few moments and dedicate them to Hashem. Remember that when you throw a pebble into a pond, there are ripples; a small act of devotion to Hashem also has ripples. The Vilna Gaon says that each *mitzvah* creates a force that propels us closer to Hashem and gives us the opportunity to do more good deeds. In the process you will find yourself feeling joyful and satisfied.

Here are some final questions to think about. It is good to ask yourself these questions once a day.

1. Do you believe that we are on earth for something more?

I once taught seventh grade. Every day when I gave them their homework assignments, they began frowning, shrieking, and jumping up and down. When they took a test, they would start crying real tears if they didn't know an answer. By December I was getting tired of all this, so I created a slogan for them: "Getting good marks is important for sure, but we are on earth for something more."

If you aren't currently studying in school, you already know that marks are not the most important thing in life. But what *is* important? Do you believe that we are on earth for something more? When you are consumed with worry, is it about details — or are you worried about giving Hashem *nachas?* In *Shaar Hada'agah* in the *Orchos Tzaddikim,* the author states that the only worry we should have is about giving Hashem happiness. So try and let go of a couple of worries.

2. Do you want to be filled with a yearning to come closer to Hashem?

When I was studying in Yerushalayim, I went to the home of one of my teachers for Shabbos. When I came in the late afternoon for *Seudah Shlishis,* I noticed that the room was shadowy. This family did not keep the lights on because there were Jews working at the electric company on Shabbos. As we sat at the table, night came over the house. I literally felt the Shabbos leaving for the first time in my life. The room became black, and the host sang a haunting tune that is still humming in my mind now: *K'ayal ta'arog...,* "As the deer thirsts for the spring of water, my soul thirsts to be close to You, Hashem."

He wasn't putting it on. He sincerely yearned to come close to Hashem.

Do you want that feeling? Some people are so numb that they can't imagine such a feeling, or they are so used to looking at life practically and realistically that they have forgotten that a sincere longing for Hashem exists. Perhaps they think that tangible faith is only for children and great *tzaddikim.* Yet it is the single most important factor in making our problems manageable.

3. Will you decide to take some time out every day to talk to Hashem ?

I found out from the following passage in *Rabbi Nachman's Wisdom* that prayer is more encompassing than I had thought: *I once had a slight need for some insignificant thing. When I mentioned it to the Rebbe, he said, "Pray to God for it." I was quite astonished to learn that one must even pray to God for such trivial things, especially in a case like this, where it was not even a necessity. Seeing my surprise, the Rebbe asked me, "Is it beneath your dignity to pray to God for a minor thing like this ?"*

The benefits of internalizing Torah concepts and of allowing yourself to experience good feelings are measureless. At first you will put in a great deal of effort, but as time goes on, you will find that you are getting more done without having to work as hard. You will find that you worry less, enjoy better health, and no longer feel helpless and alone. Your Torah outlook will improve your ability to communicate with difficult people and handle what you thought were impossible situations. You will appreciate every aspect of your life and will find yourself smiling at the most ordinary things: a baby's laughter, a fresh *challah* you have just baked, or a song your child learned in school. As Estie once told me, "I feel the glow one senses after lighting Shabbos candles — all week long."

You have the ability and the inner beauty to develop happiness from within. Don't punish yourself if it doesn't happen overnight, just keep trying. On some days you will feel naturally cheerful and at other times you will need strength to climb out of the rut. I hope that you will refer to the Torah concepts in this book again and again. Remember — a little inner joy goes a long way.

Appendix

Here is a quick-reference list of treats you can give yourself and others, as well as a "reminder" list of things to be thankful for. When you find yourself at the end of your rope, pause for a moment and look through these choices. All of them were contributed by workshop participants and are given in their own words. You are sure to find something to suit you. Whether it's an activity or simply an uplifting thought. Either way you will find yourself smiling.

I. Uplifting Treats For You

1. **Walk** — Take a brisk walk. It opens up the blood vessels and clears your head.

2. **Smile** — Make a conscious effort to smile before you say

Modeh Ani in the morning. You can't say a sincere thank-you with a sour face. It takes 72 muscles to frown and only 14 to smile.

3. **Learn** — I learn one *halachah* each morning and each evening.

4. **Set Goals** — When I first open my eyes each morning, I resolve to do Hashem's will for that day.

5. **Music** — I put on a music or lecture tape and relax on the recliner for ten minutes while I listen. Did you know that music releases endorphins, the body's natural painkillers?

6. **Telephone Visit** — I find someone to call who is in a worse position than me. Sometimes my husband, who is a doctor, asks me to give one of his patients a call.

7. **List** — I stop what I'm doing and make a list of things I've accomplished successfully.

8. **Priorities** — My father always used to say, "There are only two important things in life — Hashem's will and your health."

9. **Clear the Clutter** — I take ten minutes to put away all the clutter in the room. An uncluttered room makes my mind feel free.

10. **Gam Zu L'Tovah** — When I can't see a way out of a situation, I say *"Gam Zu L'Tovah."* I can't see the good right now, but I will see in the future that it was for the best.

11. **Personal Treasures** — I reach for treasures from the past, like a pretty fan that was given out as a memento at my wedding many years ago.

12. **Keepsakes** — I open the drawer and look at the things I have that belonged to my grandmother *a"h,* like a pearl pin and a silk scarf, and I ask myself, "How would Bubby have handled this situation?"

13. **Tehillim** — I say *Tehillim* every morning, and if I have a specific worry I say a few more chapters.

14. **Watch the Sunset** — Nature is a powerful reminder of Hashem's bounty.

15. **Hobbies** — When I am working on a sewing project, I am a different person.

16. **Photographs** — I sit down with a child and look at the family albums.

17. **Music** — My son plays the keyboard when he is bored or tense. I tell him that his music makes me feel good.

18. **Read** — I like to curl up in my favorite chair on a winter evening with a good book and a cup of warm cocoa.

19. **Talk to a Child** — I call my little nieces and talk to them. I have a great time listening to them explain things to me.

II. Small Kindnesses We Can Do For Others

Sometimes a person lives for seventy or eighty years in order to do one favor once for another Jew. Doing a kindness is so important that for the sake of one kind act Hashem will send a soul to live on earth. (*Baal Shem Tov,* quoted in *Concepts in Chassidus,* p. 47)

1. **A Shabbos Dish** — I have several neighbors who are homebound. I call them and say, "I've prepared some extra food for Shabbos. Can I stop over for a little while and bring you a little something?"

2. **Shopping** — Whenever I'm going shopping, I call a neighbor who doesn't drive and ask if she needs something.

3. **Latkes** — On Chanukah I brought latkes to an older woman who wouldn't have made them for herself. You can also offer *hamantashen* on Purim, or fruit for *Tu B'Shvat.*

4. **A Donation** — I leave some money anonymously in an envelope slipped under the door at the homes of a few people who need help twice a month.

5. **A Gift from the Block** — A family I knew really needed furniture. I raised money on the block. Together we bought beds, and we had them delivered to the family anonymously.

6. **Apologize** — I had a silly quarrel with someone I am close

to. My pride wasn't worth losing the friendship, and I apologized.

7. **Babysitting** — My twelve-year-old and ten-year-old volunteered to babysit this week for a mother who had minor surgery. Maybe we can learn something from them!

8. **Arrange a Match** — I'm a member of a group of friends who keep in touch a lot. We've decided to put our friendly conversations to good use by trying to arrange *shidduchim*. So far we have one married couple.

9. **Care Packages** — My sister moved out of town, and she's not used to the new surroundings yet. I send her letters and packages in the mail and enclose little prizes for the children.

10. **Telephone Visits** — I've put down the names and phone numbers on my wall calendar of people who are lonely, and I call one person each day.

11. **Cookies** — I took homemade cookies to a neighbor who was criticizing us a lot. Her attitude has changed significantly now.

12. **At the Door** — When my husband and children leave for work and school, I make a special effort to be at the door and send them off with a smile and a wish for a nice day.

13. **Notes** — I put encouraging notes in the children's lunchboxes. Some messages I put in — "People really like you. You are responsible. You get along well with the other kids. I'm proud of your schoolwork. You make hard things seem easy."

14. **Eye Contact** — When we speak to our children, if we can bend over closer to them and smile as we listen, we will give them a priceless gift. I'm sure that as you read this you can think of a special adult who lit up your childhood memories by talking with you in this warm way and making you feel grown-up.

15. **List** — When I was a *kallah* my teacher advised me to keep a list of nice things to say to my *chasan*. I remember actually doing it for the entire engagement period. Why not do it now?

A Good Word

Our Sages emphasize: "הַמְקַבֵּל אֶת חֲבֵרוֹ בְּסֵבֶר פָּנִים יָפוֹת אֲפִילוּ לֹא נָתַן לוֹ כְּלוּם מַעֲלֶה עָלָיו הַכָּתוּב כְּאִלוּ נָתַן לוֹ כָּל מַתָּנוֹת טוֹבוֹת שבעולם.", *"When one welcomes his friend with a smiling face and a cheerful greeting, although he has given him nothing more, the Torah considers it as though he has given him all the good gifts of this world."* Here are some familiar and not-so-familiar suggestions for spreading joy with words.

1. **"Have a Busy Day"** — When I am leaving a store, I tell the storekeeper, "Have a good day. I hope you have a busy one."

2. **"Good Afternoon"** — I used to work in the customer service department of a corporation. Now whenever I have to call a business, like the phone company, I make sure to be pleasant on the phone.

3. **"Good Night!"** — Every night I say, "I'm sorry" to any child whose feelings I hurt during the day. They also apologize. After that we both exchange thank-you's for the good things we've done for each other.

4. **"Have a Good Week"** — I call a close friend to wish her a good week. Our short conversations on *Motzai Shabbos* are a perfect way to start the week; over the phone we share a smile and throw a kiss, and then turn back to our duties. We both find strength in those few moments.

5. **"Don't Worry"** — When my neighbor boasted that she was going on vacation, I felt like saying something sarcastic, but instead I said, "Don't worry. I'll watch your house and take away the fliers, advertisements, and newspapers that pile up so that people will think you are home."

6. **"You Have Good Taste!"** — An acquaintance always wears perfectly coordinated outfits. I make sure to compliment her exquisite taste because I think her effort should be acknowledged.

7. **"Have a Good Shabbos"** — I call my husband's great aunt

every Friday to wish her a good Shabbos, and we chat for a short while. She has mentioned several times that she is happy that we consider her a part of our family.

8. **"Your Children are Polite"** — When I took my children out to eat at the pizza shop, I noticed a mother with her family of five at a nearby table. The older children were helping the younger ones, and everyone made their *berachos* out loud. Although we hadn't met before, I walked over to tell her that she was doing a marvelous job of mothering and that her children were extremely well behaved.

9. **"You Really Do That Well"** — I complimented my neighbor's home-grown tomatoes.

III. Things to be Thankful For

Here workshop participants share the everyday good things that usually pass us by before we have stopped to appreciate them.

1. **First Tooth** — My mother-in-law celebrated my daughter's first tooth by sending a donation to a yeshiva.

2. **Latkes** — Since my husband's bypass surgery, he has felt weak and has stayed in bed a lot. This morning he sat up in an easy chair, played with the grandchildren, and even made us latkes for lunch.

3. **Newspaper** — I just found out that my husband bought a Yiddish newspaper subscription for my father and sent it to his bungalow in the mountains for the entire summer.

4. **A Thoughtful Boss** — My boss called at home during a very busy moment. Instead of talking further, he graciously said, "Why don't you call me back at a convenient time in the next hour?" He saved me from being embarrassed by the background noise.

5. **A Negative Response** — I had to have a mammography

exam. The results were negative. This is one time I was so glad to hear a negative response.

6. **Cycle of Kindness** — I made *Sheva Brachos* about five years ago for someone who didn't have relatives to help her out. When she offered to buy me a gift, I said, "Someday you will make *Sheva Brachos* for someone else who needs it." Last week she did.

7. **A Snack** — My son brought me an interesting snack. It was a cup of iced tea, a tangerine, and a burger that was left from supper. I didn't really feel like eating the burger but I had to because he kept coming in to check on me and ask, "Did you finish your snack yet?" His concern was touching.

8. **Letters** — I wrote a letter to a famous author who lives in Israel and she wrote back. I love reading that letter; I know it by heart.

9. **Babies** — All I need is a smile from my infant daughter.

10. **Bird's Nest** — Today is going to be a glorious day. When I woke up, I saw a bird's nest outside my window. Can you imagine that there are beautiful bluebirds living in the middle of this crowded city?

11. **Friday Night** — I sit outside with the children and watch the men rushing to *shul* on Friday night. I say a prayer to Hashem: "Look at Your beautiful nation. They are running with all their might to serve You."

12. **Thank You** — I'm bringing a thank-you note to my co-teacher.

13. **Finding Lost Items** — My nephew went through the sock bag for me. He found ten pairs of socks, five yarmulkas, three pairs of *tzitzis* and a book I was supposed to return to his mother.

14. **Singing** — My married children came for supper last night. When all the men went to *Maariv* I sat down at the piano. My daughter-in-law and I sang duets while I played piano for half an hour.

15. **Exchanging Recipes** — I visit a friend regularly, and we always exchange recipes. I look forward to having a new dish to serve.

16. **An Apple for Mommy** — Last week, my four children went down for a snack before going to bed. My nine-year-old daughter brought me an apple that was cut into sections on a plate. I was hungry, and I really savored the apple. "Thank you so much," I said. "Well, someone has to take care of you too once in a while," she responded.

17. **The Second Shoe** — We found the second shoe! My two year old's shoe was missing for two days. She had thrown it into the dryer.

18. **Getting Some Help** — I had to run out, and I left the unfolded laundry on the couch. When I came back, I noticed that my son had folded it all and arranged the items in neat piles. It gave me such a good feeling. He just shrugged and said, "I had nothing to do and I wanted to help you out." When he saw how enthusiastic I was about the laundry, he went outside and vacuumed the car.

19. **Trust** — At a children's clothing store in Connecticut, they have a "Cash Only" policy. The Irish storekeeper said, "I'll take your check. A religious Jewish family saved my mother's life, and I trust religious Jews."

Index

About the Author

Roiza Devora Weinreich, best selling author of *There Will Never Be Another You*, has designed and presented practical workshops based on Torah principles and true success stories for the past eight years. Among the organizations she has spoken for are Ohr Somayach Alumni, Shalheves, Bais Yaakov Alumni, The Jewish Renaissance Center and Bnos Zion of Bobov. Some topics now on cassette tape are: "How To Find More Time and Energy," "Eight Things You Can Do for Your Children," and "Antidotes To Stress." If you are interested in more information or if you would like to order the weekly newsletter or the lectures on cassette tape, send a self-addressed envelope to: Roiza Weinreich, 625 Avenue L, Brooklyn, N.Y. 11230.

This volume is part of
THE ARTSCROLL SERIES®
an ongoing project of
translations, commentaries and expositions
on Scripture, Mishnah, liturgy, history,
the classic Rabbinic writings,
biographies, and thought.

For a brochure of current publications
visit your local Hebrew bookseller
or contact the publisher:

Mesorah Publications, Ltd.
4401 Second Avenue
Brooklyn, New York 11232
(718) 921-9000